A PSYCHOPATHIC PRESIDENT

Presidential Reflections…

Conformity is the jailer of freedom, and the enemy of growth." –

John F. Kennedy

One cool judgment is worth a thousand hasty counsels. The thing to be supplied is light, not heat." –

Woodrow Wilson

Any man worth his salt will stick up for what he believes right, but it takes a slightly better man to acknowledge instantly and without reservation that he is in error." –

Andrew Jackson

Keep working on a plan. Make no little plans. Make the biggest plan you can think of and spend the rest of your life carrying it out." –

Harry S. Truman

The experience of democracy is like the experience of life itself -- always changing, infinite in its variety, sometimes turbulent, and the more valuable for having been tested by adversity." –

Jimmy Carter

When angry, count 10, before you speak; if very angry, a hundred." –

Thomas Jefferson

CHAPTER 1	Revelations of first meeting
CHAPTER 2	Covert Military Strike – Middle East
CHAPTER 3	War in Central Africa
CHAPTER 4	Hamas and Hezbollah attack on strategic targets
CHAPTER 5	Russian Aggression
CHAPTER 6	Russia reneges on agreement
CHAPTER 7	US-Mexican border crisis
CHAPTER 8	School shootings shock the nation
CHAPTER 9	Hurricanes devastate Gulf of Mexico
CHAPTER 10	Presidential Elections
CHAPTER 11	Challenges domestically and internationally
CHAPTER 12	Orders to assassinate the Russian President
CHAPTER 13	Israel bombs Gaza
CHAPTER 14	Presidential scandal revealed
CHAPTER 15	Conflict in Africa
CHAPTER 16	Intimate moments with the President
CHAPTER 17	Drug Epidemic out of control
CHAPTER 18	Presidential scandal erupts
CHAPTER 19	The Assassination

CHAPTER ONE

REVELATIONS OF FIRST MEETING

Dr Eleanor Hayes was born in London, England, and was a revered psychiatrist with years of experience collaborating with individuals in the highest echelons of power, but none more important than the President of the United States of America – Daniel Trent.

As she reviewed her notes on her planned first meeting with the Commander-in-Chief, she felt uneasy. She had been appointed as a Special Adviser by senior White House staff to consult confidentially with the youngest US President to have served in office who was suffering from a stress related disorder; they worried about his decision-making ability.

The President's rise to power had been meteoric. A self-made man with a magnetic presence, he had captivated the nation with his promises of radical change. His speeches were as intoxicating as they were terrifying, laced with a charisma that made people believe in his vision and a ruthlessness that ensured his opponents were swiftly silenced.

Sitting in an outer office in the White House, Eleanor meticulously analysed the data she had gathered about the President. His public persona was immaculate—a perfect blend of confidence and empathy but beneath that veneer, she found patterns that were impossible to ignore. His charm was calculated; his empathy was an act. The real President Trent appeared manipulative, cunning, and devoid of genuine emotion. His interactions, both in public and private from the video clips she had studied, were manipulative, designed to control everyone he met, even those closest to him.

It was on record; the President's early life was in no way easy. A broken home, a series of foster placements, each one ending abruptly under mysterious circumstances. His school records showed a brilliant but volatile student, one who excelled in everything but maintained no lasting friendships.

Later, his business ventures displayed a similar pattern, fast-tracked success shadowed by ethical ambiguities and a trail of ruined lives. He was married but his wife insisted she would not undertake the formalities of the role of First Lady and would stay in the background. A revelation that told a story.

Eleanor's interviews with those who knew the President personally painted a consistent picture. His closest allies spoke of him with a mix of admiration and fear. His critics, those who were willing to speak, described encounters that were chilling in their intensity. He had a way of making people feel utterly significant and entirely disposable, often in the same breath.

As Eleanor prepared for her first face-to-face meeting with him, she knew she had to tread carefully. The stakes were immeasurably high. A psychopathic president, unrestrained and unchecked, could lead to catastrophic consequences. Her role was to understand him, to predict his moves, and to find a way to mitigate the threat he posed.

In the White House, Eleanor was led through the labyrinthine corridors to a private room, furnished tastefully but devoid of personal touches. Trent entered; he appeared a predator in a tailored suit. He greeted her with a manufactured smile; Eleanor felt the full force of his charm and the underlying menace.

"Dr Hayes," he began, "I've heard good things about you. I'm keen to see what insights you can offer. I have been under a good deal of pressure recently and suffer periodically from mild depression that I'm keen to deal with. I understand you can help, confidentially I hope?"

Eleanor matched his smile. "Thank you, Mr. President. Of course, I'm here to help in any way I can and in total confidence." The session with President Trent started cordially enough, with him projecting an air of genuine interest in her professional expertise. But Eleanor, trained to see beyond the surface, noted the expressions and subtle shifts in his manner. His eyes, though focused, had a cold detachment, and his responses were too polished, too rehearsed to be sincere.

"Your journey to the presidency has been remarkable, Mr. President," Eleanor began, steering the conversation towards his rise to power. "How did you manage to maintain such confidence and determination?"

The President leaned back, his eyes engaging hers. "Confidence comes from knowing one's abilities and understanding the landscape. Determination, well, that's a matter of necessity. When you have a vision as clear as mine, you can't afford to deviate from your goals."

Eleanor nodded, noting his response. "Your vision is indeed clear. Yet, leading a nation requires more than just vision. It requires empathy, a deep understanding of the people's needs and emotions. How do you balance these aspects?"

His smile altered a little, there was a hint he was bored by the questioning, but he answered anyway. "Empathy is about making people feel understood and valued, it's often an act. As a leader, it's my job to ensure they see that I'm working for their best interests. Sometimes, that means making tough decisions, ones they might not agree with in the moment, but will benefit from. Either way, you do what you must and without guilt or remorse."

A classic deflection in one respect and a cold admission that no matter how tough the decisions he made and their consequences he could sleep at night. She pressed on, shifting to a more personal angle. "Your background is quite compelling, Mr. President. How have your early experiences shaped your approach to leadership?"

His expression changed to philosophical. "My early life taught me resilience and adaptability. I learned that in this world, you must take control of your destiny. People sometimes suffer in your wake, but it's a price worth paying to get the job done. Those early experiences were invaluable; they made me who I am today."

Eleanor sensed an opportunity. "Control is a recurring theme in your life, it seems. Do you find it difficult to trust others, to delegate control?"

Again, The President's eyes met hers. "Trust is earned, Dr Hayes. And control is necessary to ensure things are done correctly. I've surrounded myself with competent individuals, but the responsibility is mine. If they fail in their duties they are replaced, the President cannot be seen to fail."

Eleanor held his gaze, interpreting his unspoken message. He trusted no one fully and believed in his own superiority. She shifted tactics, deciding to explore his interpersonal relationships further. "How do you maintain your relationships with those closest to you, given the immense pressures of your role?"

His smile returned, but it was more calculated. "I keep my circle tight, Dr Hayes. Those who understand me and share my vision are invaluable. Loyalty is a two-way street; I demand it, but I also reward it."

The session continued with Eleanor carefully navigating his responses, probing for more insight while maintaining a non-threatening front. Each answer added to the profile she was building, confirming her initial assessment of his psychopathic tendencies.

After the session concluded, Eleanor retreated to her office. The gravity of the situation weighed heavily on her. His psychopathic traits—his charm, manipulativeness, lack of empathy, and insatiable desire for power—were not just personality quirks; they were potential threats to national and global stability.

She began drafting her report for the senior White House team, outlining her findings and the implications of having such a personality in the highest office. This would be a confidential report and would not reach the eyes of the President. She knew she had to be strategic in how she presented this information. Directly confronting President Trent or exposing him without a solid plan could have dire consequences. Of course, she was fully aware that she had been called in to assist the President over his mental stress, not attempt to undermine his position in office.

Eleanor considered her next steps carefully. She needed allies, individuals within the administration who could understand the seriousness of her findings and help implement measures to monitor and, if necessary, curb his more dangerous impulses. It would not be easy, but she was determined to navigate it with the same determination and meticulous diligence that had defined her career.

She reached for her phone, ready to make the first call to a trusted colleague.

She called Dr James Nolan, a colleague and confidant with experience in political psychology.

As a trusted adviser to several administrations, he was someone who would grasp the gravity of her findings and offer guidance on the next steps.

"James, it's Eleanor. I need to discuss something urgent," she began.

"Eleanor, how can I help and congratulations on your new appointment."

She explained why she had been called in to consult with the President and quickly summarised her assessment of him, emphasising the psychopathic traits she had identified. James listened intently, asking pointed questions, and eventually confirming her observations with his own experiences and knowledge of Trent's public and private behaviour.

"This is potentially serious, Eleanor," James finally said. "We need to approach this delicately. You'll need a dual approach. Firstly, to agree with the President regular consultations to deal with his perceived depression, the other observing his mental capacity and potential danger to the High Office he occupies."

"I know. That's why I called you. I need a plan, one that ensures we can monitor his behaviour and mitigate potential risks without causing a political upheaval."

James agreed, and they spent the next few hours developing a strategy. They decided to create a small, discreet, task force composed of trusted individuals within the administration; people with the expertise and authority to act if necessary. This group would include members from the intelligence community, security advisers who could provide continuous assessments of his behaviour, all without the knowledge of the President.

Their first task was to gather more comprehensive data. Eleanor would arrange for regular psychological evaluations under the guise of routine health checks. These evaluations would be designed to probe deeper into his psyche without raising suspicion. Additionally, they planned to monitor his decision-making processes, looking for patterns that indicated manipulative or harmful behaviour.

Eleanor knew that gaining the trust of key members within the President's inner circle was crucial.

She needed allies who could provide insight and feedback on his use of power. She decided to contact the Vice President, Michael Reed, a seasoned politician with a reputation for integrity and pragmatism. Reed had always seemed slightly distanced from the President's more extreme rhetoric, and Eleanor hoped he would be open to her concerns.

The following day, Eleanor scheduled a private meeting with Vice President Reed. In his office, she laid out her findings, highlighting the potential dangers without causing undue alarm.

"Mr. Vice President, I believe President Trent exhibits traits consistent with psychopathy. This isn't a diagnosis I make lightly, but the implications for his decision-making and leadership are significant. I'm concerned about the potential risks to national and global stability."

Reed listened, his expression growing increasingly uneasy. "Dr Hayes, this is deeply troubling. What do you propose we do?"

"We need to monitor his behaviour closely and ensure there are safeguards in place to prevent any reckless or harmful actions. This will require a coordinated effort from trusted individuals within the administration. I believe you should play a critical role in this."

Reed nodded. "I appreciate you coming to me, Dr Hayes. This demands the utmost discretion. I'll support your efforts and help gather the necessary people for this task force."

With Reed's backing, Eleanor felt a sense of relief. Establishing the Vice President's support was a crucial step. Over the next few weeks, she and James quietly assembled their team, ensuring each member understood the delicate nature of their mission.

As the task force began its work, Eleanor continued her sessions with President Trent. Each interaction provided more data, reinforcing her initial assessment. Trent's charm remained unchanged, but Eleanor now saw it for what it was, a carefully constructed facade. She meticulously documented his responses and the subtle shifts in his behaviour, all while maintaining her professional composure. Her approach also served to support the President with his mild depression.

In the background, the task force worked to establish additional protocols for intervention. They developed scenarios and response plans for various contingencies, from erratic policy decisions to potential abuses of power. Their goal was to create a safety net that could be deployed without drawing attention or inciting panic.

One evening, after a particularly intense session with the President, Eleanor received an encrypted message from James. The intelligence community had intercepted communications suggesting that the President was planning a significant and potentially destabilising move on the international stage. The details were scant, but the implications were alarming.

Eleanor knew this was a critical moment. The task force had to act, but they needed to do so in a way that didn't expose their efforts or trigger a defensive reaction from him. She quickly arranged a meeting with James, Vice President Reed, and the key members of the task force.

In the secure confines of a high-level briefing room, they reviewed the intelligence and formulated a response. They decided to subtly delay the President's plans through bureaucratic manoeuvres and diplomatic interventions, delaying for more information to be gathered to potentially dissuade him from taking any drastic action. None of the President's plans had been discussed with the Vice President, which in itself was a worry.

Eleanor felt the weight of their mission more acutely than ever. Every move they made had to be precise, calculated, and cloaked in discretion. The stakes were high.

The tension within the White House was intense as the task force worked behind the scenes, delicately navigating the intricate web of power surrounding President Trent. Eleanor, acutely aware of the stakes, increased her efforts to understand and anticipate his moves. Her sessions with him became a careful dance, each question and observation designed to peel back the layers of his complex psyche without raising his suspicions.

During one such session, the President's facade showed cracks.

Eleanor mentioned the importance of trust and collaboration within leadership, hoping to glean more about his personal alliances and potential vulnerabilities.

"Trust is a fragile thing, Dr Hayes," Trent said, his tone revealing a rare moment of openness. "In my position, betrayal is a constant threat. That's why I keep a tight grip on the reins. I can't afford to let my guard down."

Eleanor nodded thoughtfully. "It must be exhausting, maintaining that level of control and vigilance. Do you ever feel the weight of it all?"

He paused for a moment; Eleanor saw a moment of genuine emotion—frustration or even fear. "It's a burden, but a necessary one. Weakness is not an option."

Eleanor noted this down, recognising the intense pressure he felt to maintain his dominance. It was both a source of strength and a potential Achilles' heel. She needed to use this insight to subtly influence his decisions and actions.

Meanwhile, the task force's efforts to delay the international manoeuvre bore fruit. Diplomatic channels were used to stall the President's plans, delaying for further intelligence gathering. The Vice President and other trusted allies worked behind the scenes, ensuring that critical information was rerouted, and potential crises averted. It was at that time that the President asked Eleanor to work in a strategic role with his Chief of Staff on all key matters that came to the Oval Office, giving her even more access to the President and his decision making. He valued her contribution. Of course, she accepted.

Eleanor knew that maintaining this delicate balance required constant vigilance. She decided to seek additional support from a high-ranking military official known for his integrity and strategic acumen: General Robert Whitaker. She arranged a private meeting with him, aware that gaining his cooperation could provide the task force with crucial resources and insights.

"General Whitaker," Eleanor began, "I need your help. Confidentially, The President's behaviour poses significant risks, and along with the Vice President we've formed a task force to monitor and mitigate these threats. Your expertise and position could be invaluable to our efforts."

Whitaker, a seasoned and stoic figure, listened carefully.

"Dr Hayes, I've had my own concerns about some of the President's decisions. What do you need from me?"

Eleanor explained the situation, detailing the psychological profile she had developed and the task force's strategies. She emphasised the need for a covert but effective approach, one that wouldn't trigger his paranoia or lead to retaliation.

Whitaker nodded. "I can discreetly ensure that military actions are scrutinised and delayed if necessary. We'll need to communicate securely. I trust you have measures in place for that?"

"We do," Eleanor confirmed. "And your support will make a significant difference. Thank you, General."

With Whitaker's backing, the task force's capabilities were significantly enhanced. They now had a crucial ally within the military, someone who could provide intelligence and act as a buffer against rash decisions.

CHAPTER TWO

COVERT MILITARY STRIKE MIDDLE EAST

As weeks turned into months, the task force's network of influence grew stronger. They used their combined resources to subtly shape the President's decisions, steering him away from his more destructive impulses. The intelligence community provided constant updates, allowing them to stay ahead of any potential threats.

Eleanor's sessions continued to yield valuable insights, and he seemed happy that they continued. She learned to read the subtle cues in his behaviour, understanding when he felt threatened or when he was particularly determined to pursue a risky path. Each piece of information was a tool, used to build a more comprehensive picture of the man at the helm of the nation and the world's most powerful leader.

One day, Eleanor received an urgent message from an intelligence operative. There were whispers of a coup within the administration, a faction of disgruntled officials considering drastic measures to remove the President from power. The implications were dire; any such move could plunge the country into chaos.

Eleanor convened an emergency meeting with the task force. "We need to address this immediately. A coup could destabilise everything we've worked for and lead to widespread unrest."

Vice President Reed agreed. "We need to defuse this situation without letting it spiral out of control. We must find the leaders of this faction and persuade them to stand down."

James Nolan suggested a strategy: "We can use our knowledge of the President's behaviour to our advantage. If we can show these officials that there are more effective ways to contain him, we might prevent a coup."

Eleanor proposed approaching the key figures within the faction, offering them a seat at the table in the task force. "If they see that we have a viable plan to manage him, they might be willing to join us instead of resorting to extreme measures."

The task force set to work, identifying the leaders of the coup, and arranging covert meetings. Eleanor and Vice President Reed personally met with these officials, presenting their strategy and the progress they had made.

To their relief, several key figures were persuaded. They agreed to join the task force, bringing their own resources and influence at the meetings. The threat of an immediate coup was averted.

Eleanor's resolve deepened. She knew that as long as President Trent remained in power, the task force's mission was far from over. They had to stay one step ahead, anticipating threats and protecting the nation from within. The game was complex and challenging, but Eleanor was committed to seeing it through, knowing that the safety and stability of the country depended on their success.

One afternoon, as Eleanor was reviewing the latest intelligence reports, she received an urgent call from General Whitaker.

"Dr Hayes, we have a situation," Whitaker said. "There's a military operation the President is pushing through. It's high-risk and could lead to severe international repercussions. We need to act fast."

Within the hour, the task force members were gathered in a secure location, faces tense as they absorbed the gravity of the situation.

"The President is pushing for a covert military strike on a strategic target in the Middle East," Whitaker explained. "The intelligence is shaky at best, and the potential for escalation is high. If this goes wrong, we could be looking at a significant conflict."

Vice President Reed spoke up. "We need to delay this operation without directly confronting the President If he senses obstruction, he could double down."

Eleanor nodded. "Agreed. General Whitaker, can you slow the mobilisation process? Use bureaucratic channels, logistical issues, anything that buys us time." Eleanor was rapidly drawn into the power circle as a respected thinker, and she relished the opportunity to contribute.

Whitaker nodded. "I'll manage it. We can create plausible delays."

James Nolan added, "Meanwhile, we should gather more concrete intelligence. If we can present solid evidence that the operation is too risky or unnecessary, we might sway the President's decision."

The task force went into action. Whitaker began orchestrating delays in the military planning, while intelligence operatives worked to gather and analyse data. Eleanor and Reed prepared to approach the President with their findings, carefully crafting a narrative that would appeal to his strategic sensibilities without challenging his authority.

Days passed in a blur of activity. Eleanor felt the strain of constant vigilance, but she knew they couldn't afford to falter. The stakes were too high. Finally, they had enough information to present a compelling case. Intelligence reports revealed that the target's significance had been overestimated and that a strike could destabilise the region, potentially drawing the country into a broader conflict.

Eleanor and Reed arranged a private meeting with the President. As they entered his office, the atmosphere was charged with tension.

"Mr. President, we've gathered additional intelligence regarding the proposed military operation," Reed began. "The risks are significantly higher than initially anticipated. We believe it would be wise to reconsider."

The President was irritated, but he listened as Eleanor presented the detailed findings. She emphasised the potential for collateral damage, the instability it could cause, and the long-term geopolitical consequences.

For a moment, she thought he might dismiss their concerns. But then, his expression shifted. "I appreciate your diligence; I knew your wider brief would suit you Eleanor" he said.

"This operation was intended to demonstrate strength, but if the risks are as high as you suggest, it would be wise to reassess."

Eleanor suppressed a sigh of relief. "Thank you, Mr. President. We will continue to monitor the situation and provide updates."

As they left the office, Eleanor exchanged a look with Reed. They had succeeded in averting a potentially disastrous decision, but the effort had taken its toll. Eleanor was mindful that she was taking a high-level role in a department of government that had nothing to do with her and her skill set, yet the President insisted she remain involved.

Back in her office, Eleanor allowed herself a moment to breathe. The crisis had been averted, but she knew it was only a matter of time before the next challenge arose.

In the following weeks, the task force continued to operate with meticulous precision. Eleanor's sessions with the President remained a critical source of insight. She became adept at navigating his moods, understanding when to push and when to pull back. Each interaction was a delicate balance, maintaining her professional facade while probing deeper into his psyche.

One day, during a particularly revealing session, he spoke about his childhood with an unusual degree of openness. "I learned early on that the world is a harsh place," he said, his voice almost reflective. "You either control it, or it controls you."

Eleanor used the opportunity to probe deeper. "That must have been a difficult lesson to learn at an early age. Do you ever find that this experience isolates you?"

His eyes dropped "Isolation is the price of power, Dr Hayes. It's a small price to pay for ensuring that I remain in control."

Eleanor nodded, sensing the underlying loneliness in his words. It was a rare glimpse into the vulnerability beneath his ruthless exterior. She noted it carefully, understanding that this could be a key to influencing him in the future.

As the task force continued its covert operations, they faced new challenges. The President's paranoia was growing, and he was becoming more suspicious of those around him. Eleanor and her colleagues had to adapt, finding new ways to gather intelligence and influence his decisions without triggering his defences.

Despite the constant tension, there were moments of quiet triumph. The task force managed to avert several potential crises, each success reinforcing their mission. They knew they were playing a dangerous game, but the alternative, allowing his unchecked psychopathy to dictate national and international policies was unthinkable.

One evening, as Eleanor reviewed her notes, she received a secure message from James. It contained a new piece of intelligence: a high-ranking foreign official had made contact, expressing concern about the President's unpredictable behaviour, and offering to collaborate in managing the situation.

An alliance with international partners could provide the help they needed to keep him in check. She arranged a meeting with the task force to discuss this development.

As they gathered, the mood was cautiously optimistic. "This could be a turning point," Reed said. "If we can coordinate with our allies, we'll have a stronger position to influence the President's actions."

Eleanor agreed. "We need to proceed carefully, but this could provide us with the support we need to ensure stability."

The task force began to formulate a plan for engaging with their international counterparts. They would build a network of trusted allies, to share intelligence and coordinate efforts to manage the Presidents' behaviour on a global scale.

As they worked late into the night, Eleanor knew the path was fraught with danger, but they were not alone in their efforts. With careful planning and purpose, they could protect the nation from the dangers within and ensure a safer future.

The task force's efforts to build an international alliance quickly took shape. Eleanor, Vice President Reed, and General Whitaker contacted trusted associates in allied nations, coordinating discreetly to avoid drawing the President's attention. The response was overwhelmingly positive. Leaders and officials from various countries expressed their concerns about his unpredictable behaviour reported in the media and their willingness to collaborate.

Eleanor found herself in a series of clandestine meetings and encrypted communications, working to establish a robust network of cooperation. The international partners agreed to share intelligence and provide diplomatic support, creating a united front to mitigate any rash actions by the President.

One key ally was the British Prime Minister, Olivia Bennett, who had already experienced firsthand the volatile nature of the President's leadership. In a secure video call, she emphasised the importance of a coordinated approach.

"Dr Hayes, we've seen alarming signs from President Trent's leadership. It's essential that we work together to maintain stability. Our intelligence agencies are at your disposal."

Eleanor appreciated Bennett's offer. "Prime Minister Bennett, your support is invaluable.

Eleanor's thoughts turned to her next session with the President. When they met, she steered the conversation toward his vision for the country and his upcoming plans. "Mr. President, your recent decisions have been impactful. Can you share what you had in mind for the next phase of your administration?"

His eyes shone with ambition. "The next phase will be transformative, Dr Hayes. I plan to make significant changes to ensure our nation's strength and resilience. It's time for decisive action."

Eleanor probed gently, trying to extract more details. "Decisive action can indeed bring about necessary change. What specific areas are you focusing on?"

He smiled, but it was a smile devoid of warmth. "You'll see soon enough, Dr Hayes. Sometimes, change needs to be swift and bold putting aside the perceived consequences."

His cryptic response worried her. An intercepted communication revealed that the President intended to bypass Congress with an executive order that would grant him unprecedented powers, effectively consolidating his control over key government functions.

It was a move that could dismantle the checks and balances fundamental to the democracy.

Eleanor and her colleagues coordinated with their international allies to prepare a unified response, ensuring that diplomatic channels were ready to apply pressure. Vice President Reed and key legislators began crafting legal challenges and mobilising political support to counter the executive order.

In a dramatic late-night session, the task force finalised their strategy. They would use a combination of legal, political, and diplomatic measures to delay and, if possible, block the executive order. The media would play a critical role in shaping public opinion and galvanising opposition.

The following day, as news of the impending executive order began to leak. Media outlets, tipped off by the task force, highlighted the potential dangers and rallied public sentiment against the move. Legal experts debated the constitutional elements of the President's actions, and political leaders voiced their concerns.

Eleanor watched the unfolding drama from her office. The task force's efforts were bearing fruit, but the situation was far from over. As the tension mounted, she received a message from General Whitaker. The military was on high alert, ready to intervene if necessary to prevent any misuse of power.

The next 48 hours were a whirlwind of activity. The combined pressure from legal challenges, political opposition, and international diplomacy created a formidable barrier against the executive order. Faced with mounting resistance, the President hesitated, and eventually, the order was delayed indefinitely.

CHAPTER THREE

WAR IN CENTRAL AFRICA

Eleanor and the task force had managed to avert a constitutional crisis, but the victory would be short-lived. They knew that the President's ambitions were not over, and the threat remained. He would also want to know how his plans had been leaked; totally unaware the task force existed.

Eleanor's determination deepened further. She knew that if President Trent remained in power, their vigilance could never waver. The strategy was ongoing, each move more critical than the last. But with her allies by her side, she was determined to safeguard the future from the unpredictable and potentially catastrophic impulses of Daniel Trent.

One evening, Eleanor received a cryptic message from a contact within the intelligence community. The message suggested that the President was exploring more covert methods to consolidate his power, through alliances with shadowy figures and organisations both domestically and internationally.

Eleanor immediately brought this information to the task force. "We need to understand who the President is reaching out to and what their goals are. This could be a new and dangerous escalation."

General Whitaker agreed. "We have some contacts who can provide information on these shadowy figures. We'll need to proceed with extreme caution. These are not people who take kindly to interference."

As the task force delved into this new line of inquiry, Eleanor continued her sessions with President Trent, always alert for any hint of his deeper plans. One day, he mentioned a name that sent a chill down her spine.

"I've been in discussions with some influential people, Dr Hayes. People who understand the necessity of power. One of them is Viktor Markov."

Markov was a notorious international power broker with ties to various illicit activities. His involvement suggested that the President was willing to go to extreme lengths to achieve his goals. Eleanor maintained her composure. "Viktor Markov is known for his influence. What do you hope to achieve through this alliance?"

He responded immediately. "Strength. Resilience. The ability to act decisively without the constraints of bureaucracy. Markov and his associates can provide resources and support that are beyond the reach of conventional means."

Eleanor knew she had to relay this information immediately.

The task force mobilised its resources, using international contacts and intelligence networks to gather information on Markov and his associates. They discovered that Markov participated in a range of activities, from arms dealing to cyber espionage, all aimed at destabilising governments and expanding his influence.

With this new intelligence, the task force developed a multi-pronged strategy. They would expose Markov's activities to international authorities, disrupt his operations, and use diplomatic channels to pressure his allies. Simultaneously, they would work to cut off the President's access to people like Markov.

Eleanor and General Whitaker coordinated closely with international partners. British Prime Minister Bennett and other leaders were instrumental in rallying support for a concerted effort to stop Markov's influence. Together, they launched a series of covert operations to dismantle Markov's networks and disrupt his financial streams.

As the task force intensified its efforts, the President's frustration grew. He sensed resistance but couldn't pinpoint its source. Eleanor continued to play her role, offering counsel and insight while subtly guiding him away from his most dangerous impulses.

Eleanor received a coded message from an intelligence contact in Eastern Europe. They had successfully intercepted a significant arms shipment intended for one of Markov's factions. The disruption was a major blow to Markov's operations and sent a clear signal that his activities were being closely monitored.

Eleanor shared the news with the task force. "This is a significant victory. We've cut off one of Markov's key resources. But we need to remain vigilant. The President will not give up easily."

In the following weeks, the task force's efforts bore fruit. Markov's influence waned, and the President's ability to access covert resources was severely restricted. International partners stepped up their cooperation, creating a formidable alliance that could counter any further attempts by him to consolidate power through illicit means.

Eleanor's noticed subtle changes in the President's attitude, a growing frustration, and a sense of isolation. He was beginning to feel the pressure, and Eleanor knew this could be both a danger and an opportunity.

One day, he spoke with uncharacteristic vulnerability. "Sometimes I wonder if it's worth it, Dr Hayes. The constant struggle, the battles on every front. Power is a lonely place."

Eleanor responded. "Power can be isolating, Mr. President. But leadership is not just about control; it's about trust and collaboration. The strongest leaders are those who build bridges, not walls."

He considered her words. For a moment, Eleanor saw a flicker of doubt in his eyes. It was a small opening, but it gave her hope that, with time and careful influence, they could steer him toward a more balanced approach.

A war had broken out in Central Africa, to do with precious metal mining rights, and despite officials advising the President to avoid comment or involvement, he called one of the rebel leaders directly and pledged military support and hardware.

Eleanor was stunned when she heard the news. The implications of his unilateral decision were staggering. Not only had he committed the nation to a foreign conflict without consulting Congress or his advisers, but he had also sided with a faction known for its human rights abuses and ties to illicit activities. This reckless move threatened to destabilise the entire region and entangle the country in a conflict with significant moral and political repercussions.

The task force quickly convened to assess the situation. General Whitaker's expression was grim as he reviewed the intelligence reports. "This is a disaster waiting to happen. The President's support for the rebels could trigger an international crisis."

James Nolan added, "We need to understand the full scope of this commitment. What kind of military support has he promised? And how soon will it be delivered?"

Eleanor nodded. "We also need to gather as much information as we can about the rebel leader he contacted. Who is he, and what are their true intentions?"

Vice President Reed, who had become increasingly involved in the task force's efforts, spoke up. "We should reach out to our allies in the region. They might have additional intelligence and could help us mitigate the fallout from this decision."

As the team delved into their research, they discovered that the rebel leader the President had contacted was a ruthless warlord named General Abasi. General Abasi had a notorious reputation for exploiting mining rights, using child soldiers, and committing widespread atrocities. His faction controlled significant territories rich in precious metals, making them a powerful but controversial force in the ongoing conflict.

Eleanor used diplomatic channels and intelligence agencies in neighbouring countries, seeking any intelligence they had on General Abasi and his operations. The responses were alarming. Reports confirmed that Abasi's forces were guilty of numerous war crimes, and his alliance with the President could draw international condemnation and severe diplomatic repercussions.

Meanwhile, General Whitaker coordinated with military and intelligence officials to track any movement of arms or personnel that might indicate the beginning of the President's promised support. "We need to intercept any shipments and prevent this from escalating further," he urged.

Eleanor knew they needed to act quickly. She arranged a meeting with Vice President Reed and key members of Congress who were equally alarmed by the situation. "We have to present a united front," she insisted. "We need to show that the President's actions do not reflect the will of our government and that we are committed to peace and stability in the region."

The task force also reached out to international media outlets, providing them with detailed reports on General Abasi's human rights abuses. They hoped to generate public outrage and pressure on the President to back away from his support. The story quickly gained traction, with headlines highlighting the brutal nature of the rebel faction and questioning the President's judgement.

Amidst this flurry of activity, Eleanor met with him.

"Mr. President, the situation in Central Africa is complex and fraught with danger. Our involvement could have serious repercussions both internationally and domestically. Have you considered the potential fallout from this decision?" She knew she was on thin ice.

His eyes flashed with frustration. "Dr Hayes, I made a promise to support a cause that I believe in. These rebels are fighting against corruption and exploitation. They need our help."

Eleanor gave a thoughtful response. "I understand your desire to support justice, but there are reports indicating that General Abasi's forces have committed serious atrocities. Our support for them could damage our credibility and lead to further instability."

"With respect Dr Hayes, this is not your area of expertise. "Sometimes, difficult choices are necessary. We can't always sit on the sidelines."

Seeing that direct confrontation was futile, Eleanor decided to take a different approach. "We could explore alternative ways to support the region. Humanitarian aid, diplomatic efforts, and collaborating with international partners to broker peace. There are ways to make a positive impact without escalating the conflict."

He was silent for a moment, and Eleanor hoped that she had planted a seed of doubt. She knew it would take time and persistent effort to change his mind, but she was determined to try.

Back in the task force's war room they successfully intercepted a shipment of arms meant for General Abasi's forces, dealing a significant blow to his military capabilities. International pressure mounted, with world leaders condemning the President's actions and urging him to reconsider his support for the rebels.

The situation remained tense, but the task force's efforts were beginning to pay off. Several high-ranking officials within the administration started to voice their concerns. The President found himself increasingly isolated, facing mounting resistance both domestically and internationally.

Eleanor continued her delicate dance, providing counsel while subtly guiding him away from his most dangerous impulses. She knew there were tough times ahead, but with each small victory, there was a glimmer of hope. The task force had proven that through strategic collaboration they could have influence, even in the face of immense challenges.

As the weeks went by, the combined pressure from the task force, international community, and domestic opposition forced him to reconsider his position. Reluctantly, he announced a change of commitment to the Central African conflict, signalling a potential shift in policy.

Despite the temporary reprieve, the atmosphere in the White House remained tense. General Abasi's forces were still a significant threat, and the President's initial pledge of support had already given confidence to the warlord. Eleanor and her team knew they needed a more comprehensive strategy to prevent further escalation and stabilise the region.

The task force gathered more intelligence on Abasi's operations and identified potential weaknesses. They also sought to build a consensus with international partners willing to intervene diplomatically and, if necessary, militarily, to neutralise the threat posed by Abasi's faction.

Eleanor reached out to key allies in Europe and Africa, arranging high-level meetings to discuss a coordinated response. British Prime Minister Bennett and other world leaders expressed their deep concerns but were also willing to collaborate on a solution.

"We must act decisively," Bennett said during one such meeting. "General Abasi cannot be allowed to continue his reign of terror. If we stand together, we can exert the necessary pressure to bring him to the negotiating table and secure a lasting peace."

Eleanor agreed. "We need a multifaceted approach that includes diplomatic pressure, targeted sanctions, and, if necessary, military intervention. Our goal should be to isolate Abasi and force him to reconsider his actions without causing further harm to the civilian population."

Meanwhile, within the United States, the political landscape was shifting. The President's support base began to erode as more details about General Abasi's atrocities became public. Congress initiated hearings to investigate the President's actions, and several prominent lawmakers called for a review of the country's foreign policy.

Vice President Reed played a crucial role in these efforts, using his influence to rally support for a more measured and ethical approach. He worked closely with the task force to draft a comprehensive plan that would address the crisis in Central Africa while upholding the nation's commitment to human rights and international law.

During a crucial meeting, Reed outlined the plan. "We will propose a resolution in Congress to condemn General Abasi's actions and authorise a humanitarian intervention. At the same time, we'll collaborate with our international partners to implement targeted sanctions against Abasi's regime to cut off his resources."

General Whitaker nodded in agreement. "Our military is prepared to provide logistical support for humanitarian operations and, if necessary, enforce a no-fly zone to protect civilians from further violence. But we must ensure that any military action is part of a broader strategy that prioritises diplomacy and long-term stability."

The task force engaged with non-governmental organisations and humanitarian groups to coordinate aid efforts for the affected region. Eleanor knew that winning the hearts and minds of the local population was crucial to any lasting peace, and she wanted to ensure that their efforts were seen as a genuine attempt to help, not as another instance of foreign interference.

CHAPTER FOUR

HAMAS AND HEZBOLLAH PLAN ATTACK ON STRATEGIC TARGETS

As the weeks passed, the task force's strategy took shape. Congress passed the resolution, and international partners pledged their support for the humanitarian intervention. Sanctions against General Abasi's regime were swiftly implemented, and diplomatic efforts to isolate him intensified.

On the ground in Central Africa, the situation remained precarious, but there were signs of progress. Humanitarian aid began to reach displaced civilians, and local leaders started to voice their support for the international coalition's efforts. Eleanor and her team monitored developments closely, adjusting their strategy as needed to respond to the rapidly changing dynamics.

Eleanor continued her sessions with President Trent.

"Mr. President, our commitment to Central Africa must be guided by our values and our responsibility to protect human lives. General Abasi's actions are indefensible, and our support for his regime undermines everything we stand for."

The President looked weary the weight of his decisions evident on his face. "I thought supporting the rebels would bring about change, but I see now that it's more complicated than that."

She was encouraged by his remark. "It's not too late to change course. By working with our allies and supporting a humanitarian approach, we can still make a positive impact. True leadership is about recognising when change is necessary and implementing it."

With his tentative agreement, Eleanor felt a sense of relief. He never asked how his plans had been leaked but discovered acting independently could bring down his Presidency.

General Abasi found himself increasingly isolated. His forces, deprived of the promised support from the President and facing mounting pressure from the international community, began to fracture. Diplomatic efforts to broker a ceasefire gained traction, and there were tentative signs that a negotiated settlement might be possible.

Eleanor and the task force knew the situation could change at any moment. They continued to gather intelligence, monitor developments, and adapt their strategies to ensure that peace and stability could be achieved.

The task force's success in navigating this complex crisis reaffirmed their belief in the power of strategic collaboration. They had faced immense challenges, but through their collective efforts, they had managed to steer the nation away from a potentially catastrophic path chosen by the President. Although the immediate crisis had been averted, the region remained fragile, and the potential for further conflict was ever-present. They had to maintain their vigilance and continue working towards a long-term solution that would bring lasting stability to Central Africa.

Eleanor and her team focused on maintaining the alliances they had formed ensuring that the support for the humanitarian effort remained strong. They worked closely with international organisations that addressed not only the immediate needs of the displaced populations but also the underlying issues that had fuelled the conflict.

Meanwhile, the diplomatic efforts to broker a ceasefire continued. Eleanor's diplomatic skills were put to the test as she navigated the complex negotiations, always aware of the delicate balance needed to achieve a sustainable agreement.

One day, Eleanor received a message from one of her intelligence contacts. There were rumours that General Abasi was growing increasingly desperate. His forces were dwindling, and his support base was eroding. Some of his top lieutenants were defecting, and there was a possibility that Abasi might be willing to negotiate a surrender.

Eleanor circulated this information to the task force. "This could be the breakthrough we've been waiting for. If we can persuade Abasi to surrender, it would significantly reduce the violence and pave the way for a lasting peace."

General Whitaker was cautious. "We need to be careful. Abasi is a cunning and ruthless leader. He might be using this as a ploy to delay or to regroup his forces."

Vice President Reed agreed. "We should approach this with a combination of firmness and flexibility. Offer him a way out but make it clear that any further aggression will be met with a decisive response."

A plan was developed to reach out to Abasi through back channels, offering him a chance to surrender in exchange for safe passage and a guarantee of fair treatment under international law. They also made it clear that continued resistance would result in increased military pressure and further isolation.

As the negotiations progressed, Eleanor had further sessions with President Trent, keeping him informed of their efforts and seeking his support for the task force's strategy. His attitude had softened since their last conversation, and he seemed more open to the idea of a diplomatic resolution.

"Dr Hayes, if General Abasi is willing to surrender, we must ensure that the transition is managed carefully. We can't afford to create a power vacuum that could lead to more chaos," he said during one of their meetings.

Eleanor nodded. "Agreed, Mr. President. Our goal is to stabilise the region and create conditions for sustainable peace. This means supporting legitimate governance structures and ensuring that humanitarian aid reaches those who need it most."

The breakthrough came sooner than expected. General Abasi, facing mounting pressure from both within his ranks and from the international community, agreed to a ceasefire and expressed his willingness to negotiate a surrender. The task force moved quickly to formalise the agreement, working with regional leaders to ensure that the terms were fair and that the transition would be as smooth as possible.

The news of Abasi's surrender was met with cautious optimism around the world. The task force had managed to defuse a potentially explosive situation, but they knew that the challenging work was just beginning.

The region's recovery would require sustained effort and support from the international community.

Eleanor and her team coordinated with international aid agencies to deliver food, medical supplies, and other essential resources to the affected areas. They also supported efforts to rebuild infrastructure, promote economic development, and strengthen governance institutions knowing this would take time.

One evening, as she reviewed the latest reports from Central Africa, Eleanor received a call from one of her contacts in the intelligence community. There was added information suggesting that a group of US disaffected military officers were plotting to undermine the task force's efforts.

Eleanor's heart sank. She had always known that the fight to protect the nation from within was far from over, but this news underscored just how precarious their situation remained. She immediately convened an emergency meeting of the task force to discuss the threat.

"This is a serious development," General Whitaker said. "If there are elements within the military that are actively working against us, we need to identify them stop the threat before it escalates."

Vice President Reed added, "We also need to ensure that President Trent is kept informed and on our side. Any hint of internal division could be exploited by our enemies."

Eleanor agreed. "We need to act swiftly and decisively. I'll continue my sessions with the President and try to gauge his reaction to this news. In the meantime, we need to gather as much information as possible about this plot and develop a plan to counter it."

The task force sprang into action, using their extensive network of contacts and resources to investigate. They worked discreetly, aware that any leak could tip off the conspirators and trigger a premature confrontation.

During her next session with the President, Eleanor broached the topic delicately.

"Mr. President, I've received some concerning information. There are elements within the military that may be plotting against our efforts to stabilise Central Africa and could pose a threat to your administration."

He considered her words carefully. "What do you propose we do?"

Eleanor paused for a moment. "We need to strengthen our internal security measures and identify the key players involved. At the same time, we must continue our efforts to stabilise Central Africa and demonstrate to the world that we are committed to peace and justice." It was obvious from his reaction he was not implicated or encouraged the plot.

The President nodded slowly. "I'll authorise whatever resources you need. This nation cannot afford to be divided at such a critical time."

With his support, the task force redoubled their efforts. They identified several high-ranking officers who were suspected of being involved and monitored their activities closely. Through a combination of intelligence gathering and strategic pressure, they managed to neutralise the threat before it could fully materialise.

Once again, tensions were rising in the Middle East, a region the President knew well. As a Senator, he had been influential in calming tensions and had visited the territory several times. It became clear that Hamas and other militia groups funded and encouraged by Iran were conspiring, but intelligence had not uncovered what they had planned.

Eleanor received the latest brief from the intelligence community. The reports were concerning increased communications between Hamas leaders and Iranian officials, unexplained movements of militia groups, and heightened rhetoric in the region. Yet, the exact nature of their plans remained elusive.

Eleanor called an emergency meeting of the task force. "We need to understand what Hamas and their allies are planning," she said. "If we don't, we risk being confronted by another crisis."

General Whitaker nodded. "Our contacts in the region might have some insight. We need to intensify our intelligence operations and use our alliances to get a clearer picture."

Vice President Reed added, "We should also consider diplomatic channels. President Trent's history in the Middle East could be an asset. If he can reestablish some of those old connections, it might give us a way to de-escalate the situation before it escalates further."

Eleanor agreed. "I'll speak with the President. We need to approach this from all angles.

Later that day, Eleanor met with President Trent. She found him in a reflective mood, staring at a map of the Middle East on his office wall. "Mr. President, we have credible intelligence that suggests Hamas and other groups possibly Hezbollah are planning something significant, with Iran's backing. We don't know what their plans are, but it's critical we find out."

He turned to her. "I've been to the region many times. I know the players, the history, the stakes. This could be an opportunity to leverage those connections, but we need to tread carefully."

Eleanor nodded. "We need your experience and your influence Mr President. Reaching out to old allies, opening diplomatic channels, it could have influence. We also need to ramp up our intelligence efforts on the ground and ensure our regional partners are fully engaged."

The President agreed. "I'll start making calls. We need to show strength but also offer a path to peace."

As President Trent reconnected with key figures in the Middle East, Eleanor and the task force intensified their intelligence operations. They collaborated with allies in Israel, Jordan, and Saudi Arabia, sharing information and coordinating efforts to uncover the militia groups' plans.

One evening, Eleanor received a message from an Israeli intelligence contact. They had intercepted communications suggesting that a large-scale attack was being planned, targeting multiple locations across the region, including key American interests. The timing and specifics were still unclear, but the threat was imminent.

Eleanor immediately convened the task force. "We have a credible threat," she announced. "Multiple targets, including American interests. We need to act fast."

General Whitaker outlined the military's readiness to respond. "Our forces in the region are on high alert. We can deploy additional assets if needed, but we need precise intelligence to ensure we're not reacting to a false alarm."

Vice President Reed emphasised the importance of diplomacy. "We should coordinate with our allies and ensure they're prepared. At the same time, we need to communicate to Iran and its proxies that any attack will be met with a decisive response."

President Trent's diplomatic efforts began to bear fruit. He managed to secure commitments from key regional leaders to cooperate in averting the crisis. He also sent a direct message to Iran through intermediaries, warning of severe consequences if any attacks were conducted.

As the intelligence community continued to piece together the details of the planned attack, Eleanor received a call from one of her contacts within the CIA. "We've located a key figure in Hamas who might have the information we need. If we can apprehend him, we might be able to uncover the full extent of their plans."

Eleanor relayed the information to General Whitaker. "We need to act quickly. This could be our best chance to prevent the attack."

A covert operation was swiftly planned and executed. The task force, working with Israeli special forces, successfully captured the Hamas operative. Under interrogation, he revealed critical details about the planned attacks, including the targets and timing.

Armed with this information, the task force coordinated a series of pre-emptive strikes and security measures to neutralise the threat. Key militia leaders were apprehended, weapons caches were destroyed, and the planned attacks were stopped.

In the aftermath, President Trent addressed the nation.

"Through the combined efforts of our intelligence community, our military, and our allies, we have averted a significant threat to peace and stability in the Middle East. This success is a testament to the power of collaboration and the importance of vigilance."

Eleanor and the task force had done their job. They had managed to prevent a major crisis, but the experience showed the ever-present danger posed by groups like Hamas and their backers in Iran.

As the team debriefed, General Whitaker remarked, "This was a close call. We need to stay ahead of these threats and continue strengthening our intelligence and diplomatic networks."

Vice President Reed agreed. "And we need to keep building on the relationships we've established. President Trent's connections in the region were invaluable. We need to ensure that those ties remain strong and that we continue to work together to maintain stability."

Eleanor nodded, knowing that the President had been an asset on this occasion but could so easily be a liability on the throw of a dice.

The situation in Ukraine had reached a critical point. Russian military attacks had intensified, targeting key locations with devastating precision, and now Kyiv was under extreme threat of serious bombardment, forcing the population to flee. The world watched in horror as the humanitarian crisis escalated.

President Trent convened a high-level meeting with his senior advisers, including Eleanor Hayes, General Whitaker, and Vice President Reed. The room was tense, the gravity of the situation undisputed. The President's expression was determined as he addressed his team.

"We have stood by for too long, watching Russia gain confidence and expand its aggression," he began. "It's time for decisive action. I am prepared to issue a Presidential order for an attack on Russian forces in Ukraine. The United States must intervene to end this war and restore peace."

Eleanor's jaw dropped. Direct military involvement in Ukraine could have far-reaching and unpredictable consequences.

She knew that while his intentions were to protect and stabilise, the risks of escalation with Russia were immense.

"Mr. President," Eleanor said carefully, "we need to consider the potential repercussions. Direct military engagement with Russian forces could lead to a broader conflict, even drawing in NATO and escalating into a full-scale war."

General Whitaker spoke up. "We need to weigh all options, including the readiness of our forces, the potential for civilian casualties, and the international response. We have allies who will support us, but we also have to anticipate significant retaliation from Russia and its partners."

Vice President Reed added, "Diplomatic channels should be a priority. There may still be opportunities to pressure Russia through economic sanctions, cyber operations, and international isolation. Ground troops should be a last resort."

The President listened but remained committed to his idea. "I understand the risks, but we cannot allow Russia to continue its unchecked aggression. The Ukrainian people need our help, and our allies are looking to us for leadership. We will proceed with preparations, but we will also ramp up our diplomatic efforts to bring Russia to the negotiating table."

The task force was mobilised to develop a comprehensive plan. They needed to prepare for all contingencies, ensuring that military, diplomatic, and humanitarian strategies were aligned.

Eleanor worked closely with intelligence agencies to gather the latest information on Russian troop movements and military capabilities. She also reached out to international partners, coordinating efforts to apply maximum pressure on Russia through sanctions and diplomatic channels.

General Whitaker oversaw the military preparations. Troops were put on high alert, and strategic assets were repositioned to support potential operations in Ukraine. The goal was to be ready for any eventuality while maintaining a stance that could deter further Russian aggression.

Vice President Reed led the diplomatic offensive.

He engaged with NATO allies, reinforcing the message that the US was committed to protecting Ukraine and ensuring regional stability. He also cooperated with European leaders to craft a unified response that combined military readiness with robust economic sanctions.

As the preparations got underway, Eleanor continued her sessions with President Trent emphasising the need for a balanced approach. "Mr. President, our goal should be to compel Russia to withdraw through a combination of force and diplomacy. We must be prepared to act, but primarily to negotiate."

He nodded. "I agree, Dr Hayes. We will show strength, but we will also leave the door open for a peaceful resolution. You have come a long way. You get diplomacy!"

Of course, she had matured in the job and was now considered a valuable asset within the President's inner circle, but she worried the President hadn't grasped the value of diplomacy as she had.

The tension in Ukraine continued to escalate. Reports of civilian casualties and widespread destruction filled the news, adding urgency to the task force's efforts. The international community was on edge, watching closely to see how the US would respond.

CHAPTER FIVE

RUSSIAN AGRESSION

One evening, Eleanor received a coded message from a trusted contact within the Russian government. The message hinted at cracks within the Kremlin's inner circle; some Russian officials were becoming increasingly uneasy about the war's direction and the potential for catastrophic escalation.

Eleanor brought this information to the task force. "We might have an opportunity here. If we can exploit these internal divisions within Russia, we could potentially force them to the negotiating table without a full-scale military confrontation."

General Whitaker saw the potential. "We could use psychological operations combined with our show of military readiness. It might create enough pressure to force a change in their strategy."

Vice President Reed agreed. "We need to communicate clearly that continued aggression will only lead to greater isolation and economic hardship for Russia. We can leverage our diplomatic channels to reinforce this message."

President Trent approved the plan. "Let's move forward. Prepare our troops but also increase our diplomatic and psychological operations. We need to show Russia that their path is untenable." They all knew that a growing alliance was emerging of Russia, Iran, North Korea, and China who recognised that US influence internationally was waning.

Over the next few days, the task force executed their multi-faceted strategy. They intensified diplomatic efforts, pushing for stronger sanctions and gathering international support. At the same time, they conducted targeted psychological operations aimed at sowing discord within the Russian leadership.

The US military maintained a high state of readiness, conducting exercises that demonstrated their capability to intervene if necessary.

This show of strength was coupled with backchannel communications to Russian officials, emphasising the catastrophic consequences of continued aggression.

The combined pressure began to have an effect. Reports from within Russia indicated growing dissent among military and political leaders. The economic impact of the sanctions was starting to bite, and public opinion was becoming increasingly restless.

In a surprising turn of events, a high-ranking Russian official made contact through intermediaries, expressing a willingness to engage in peace talks. The message was clear: Russia was looking for a way out without losing face.

President Trent authorised a special envoy to begin preliminary discussions, while the task force continued to apply pressure on all fronts.

As negotiations progressed, the situation in Ukraine began to stabilise. The threat of a new bombardment of Kyiv receded, and humanitarian aid started to flow more freely into the affected areas.

In a landmark moment, representatives from the US, Ukraine, Russia, and key international partners convened for peace talks. The negotiations were complex, but after several days of intense discussion, a tentative agreement was reached.

Russia agreed to a phased withdrawal of its forces from Ukraine, in exchange for an immediate easing of some economic sanctions and security assurances for its interests in the region. The agreement included provisions for international monitoring and support for rebuilding efforts in Ukraine.

President Trent addressed the nation, highlighting the collaborative efforts that had led to this breakthrough. "Today, we have taken a significant step towards peace in Ukraine. This agreement is a testament to the power of US diplomacy. We will continue to support Ukraine and work towards a stable and secure future for the region."

As the task force reflected, they knew that this achievement could be short-lived.

The complexities of international relations and the ever-present threat of aggression demanded constant vigilance.

Less than a week later, drones detected a massive new mobilisation of Russian ground forces and military hardware on the border of Ukraine, defying the recently agreed accord. The news spread rapidly, causing global anxiety as it became evident that Russia was prepared to sideline the US President and escalate the conflict.

Eleanor received the urgent intelligence report and immediately convened the task force. The atmosphere was tense as they gathered to discuss what to do.

"We have clear evidence that Russia is mobilising its forces again," Eleanor began. "This is a blatant violation of the accord and a direct challenge to our efforts for peace."

General Whitaker's expression was grim. "We need to respond decisively. This mobilisation could signal an imminent ramping up of military effort, and we must be prepared to counter it."

Vice President Reed agreed. "We need to coordinate with our allies immediately and issue a strong warning to Russia. At the same time, we must increase our military readiness and consider additional sanctions."

President Trent, who had joined the meeting via secure video link, was visibly frustrated. "We can't allow this to go unchallenged. It's clear that Russia is testing our resolve. We need to send a message that their actions will have severe consequences. I said only recently that we should attack Russian forces on Ukrainian territory. This must remain on the table."

The task force quickly formulated a multi-pronged response. Eleanor was tasked with coordinating the diplomatic offensive, while General Whitaker focused on military preparedness. Vice President Reed would lead the efforts to rally international support for a unified response.

Eleanor contacted key international partners to share the intelligence. She emphasised the need for a strong, unified stance to deter further Russian aggression.

In parallel, General Whitaker ordered the US military to increase its presence in Eastern Europe. Additional troops and equipment were deployed to NATO bases, and joint military exercises took place to demonstrate to the Russian's that they were serious.

Vice President Reed engaged with European leaders, pushing for a new round of stringent economic sanctions against Russia. The goal was to isolate Russia economically and diplomatically, making it clear that continued aggression would come at a high cost.

As these efforts unfolded, President Trent prepared to address the nation and the international community. He needed to convey the seriousness of the situation and that the United States would uphold international law and support Ukraine.

In a nationally televised address, President Trent spoke directly to the American people and the world. "Less than two weeks ago, we achieved a significant diplomatic breakthrough for peace in Ukraine. Today, we face a grave challenge as Russia has chosen to violate that accord and mobilise its forces once again. The United States, together with our allies, will not stand idly by. We will respond with strength to protect the sovereignty of Ukraine and uphold the principles of international law."

The response from the international community was swift. NATO allies pledged additional support, and a new round of economic sanctions targeting key sectors of the Russian economy, and individuals close to the Russian President. The message was clear: Russia's actions would not go unpunished.

As the world watched the unfolding crisis, Eleanor and the task force remained in constant communication, analysing intelligence, and coordinating efforts. They knew that the situation was precarious and could lead to a full-scale conflict.

In a strategic move, President Trent authorised a covert operation to gather more detailed intelligence on the Russian mobilisation. Special forces were deployed to gather real-time information on troop movements and military capabilities, providing crucial insights for the task force's planning.

Eleanor received updates from the field, piecing together a clearer picture of Russia's intentions. The intelligence suggested that the mobilisation was not merely a show of force but serious preparation for a large-scale incursion into Ukraine, larger than had been previously seen.

With this information, diplomatic channels were used to convey clear warnings to Russia, emphasising the dire consequences of further aggression. At the same time, military preparations continued, ensuring that US and NATO forces were ready to respond if necessary.

Eleanor received a message from a trusted source within the Russian government. The source indicated that there were significant divisions within the Kremlin about the wisdom of escalating the conflict. Some officials were deeply concerned about the economic and diplomatic fallout of a prolonged confrontation with the West.

Eleanor brought this information to the task force. "We might have an opportunity to exploit these internal divisions within Russia," she said. "If we can amplify these concerns and apply additional pressure, we might be able to force a reconsideration of their aggressive stance."

General Whitaker agreed. "We should intensify our psychological operations, further targeting key figures within the Russian leadership. At the same time, we need to maintain our military and diplomatic offensive."

Vice President Reed added, "We must encourage our allies to increase their economic pressure. The more isolated and economically effected Russian people feel, the more likely their leadership will back down."

Covert operations targeted the Russian leadership with disinformation and psychological tactics designed to create doubt and conflict. Simultaneously, diplomatic efforts and economic sanctions were ramped up, increasing the pressure on Russia from multiple angles.

As the days passed, signs of strain within the Russian government became more apparent. Reports of high-level disagreements and public dissent emerged, suggesting that the task force's strategy was having an impact.

In a surprising turn of events, a faction within the Russian government covertly contacted international intermediaries, indicating a willingness to de-escalate the situation. They proposed renewed talks to address the underlying issues and find a path to peace.

President Trent agreed, authorising his special envoy to engage in preliminary discussions. The task force continued to monitor the situation closely, ready to respond to any developments.

The renewed negotiations were complex and fraught with tension, but the combined pressure from military readiness, economic sanctions, and diplomatic efforts created an environment for progress. Gradually, a new framework for peace began to take shape.

In an historic announcement, President Trent addressed the world. "Through steadfast resolve and the combined efforts of our allies, we have once again brought Russia to the negotiating table. This agreement represents a renewed commitment to peace and stability in Ukraine. We will continue to support Ukraine and uphold the principles of international law."

A week later, the Russians reneged on their commitments, launching another devastating bombardment on Kyiv that resulted in the deaths of hundreds of innocent civilians. The images of destruction and loss were broadcast worldwide, igniting outrage. Eleanor knew that President Trent would be enraged by this latest act of aggression and feared he might act irrationally in retaliation. She needed to reach him urgently to plead for restraint.

Eleanor immediately contacted James Nolan, the President's Chief of Staff, to arrange an emergency meeting. "James, we need to meet with the President before he makes any hasty decisions. The consequences could be catastrophic."

Nolan, who shared Eleanor's concerns, agreed to set up the meeting. "I'll get you in as soon as possible, Eleanor. He's already furious and talking about immediate military action."

Within the hour, Eleanor found herself in the Oval Office with President Trent, Vice President Reed, General Whitaker, and other senior advisers.

The President was angry as he reviewed the latest intelligence reports and casualty figures.

"Eleanor, you wanted to speak with me," he said, his tone barely controlled.

"Mr. President, I understand your anger and frustration. What Russia has done is reprehensible and demands a response. However, we must act with a clear strategy to avoid further escalation that could lead to a broader conflict."

He looked at Eleanor and shook his head. "They've slaughtered innocent people, Eleanor. We can't just sit back and do nothing. They need to know that there are consequences for their actions."

General Whitaker nodded in agreement. "We can strike key military targets in Russia to cripple their capabilities and send a strong message. We have the means to conduct precision strikes that will minimise civilian casualties."

Vice President Reed offered a note of caution. "While we must respond, we also need to consider the broader implications. A direct attack on Russian territory could provoke a severe and nuclear retaliation. We must ensure that any action we take doesn't spiral out of control."

Eleanor used the moment to build on Reed's point. "Mr. President, we need a multifaceted approach. Military action should be on the table, but let's also consider cyber operations to disrupt their command and control, as well as additional sanctions to further destabilise their economy. We can rally our allies to further isolate Russia diplomatically and economically."

The President's expression remained steadfast as he listened to the balanced arguments. "What you propose Dr Hayes won't stop the Russian's. It is only direct force that will change their minds, you must all see that?" Eleanor remained composed.

"We need to show strength, but also maintain our strategic advantage," Eleanor continued.

"First, I think you should authorise a cyber offensive to disrupt Russian military operations and communications. Second, impose the harshest sanctions yet targeting their energy sector and key financial institutions. Third, work with our NATO allies to increase military presence in Eastern Europe, sending a clear signal of our commitment to Ukraine. Finally, initiate a covert operation to support Ukrainian resistance forces."

General Whitaker added, "We can deploy additional missile defence systems in Ukraine to protect against further airstrikes. This will not only save lives but also bolster Ukrainian defences."

The President considered the advice. "Alright, we'll go with this comprehensive approach. Prepare the cyber offensive, escalate the sanctions, and increase our military presence. General, I want missile defence systems in Ukraine within the week. And let's start coordinating with our allies immediately, but I want to make it clear I am not taking direct action off the table."

Eleanor felt a sense of relief as the meeting concluded. The President had chosen a measured, strategic response that balanced the need for action avoiding uncontrolled escalation, however, she knew the situation remained extremely volatile, and the President's support could waver or worst still lead him to follow his disastrous instinct that 'troops on the ground' would be the cure.

Over the next few days, the task force worked to implement the President's directives. Cyber units launched operations to disrupt Russian military communications, causing confusion and delays in their operations. The new round of sanctions targeted Russia's energy exports and financial transactions that would increase the economic pressure on the Kremlin. NATO allies began to move additional troops and equipment to Eastern Europe, bolstering defences and demonstrating solidarity.

Eleanor maintained communication with international partners, ensuring a coordinated and unified response. She also kept a close watch on President Trent, offering counsel and support to help him navigate the intense pressure of the crisis.

The situation in Ukraine remained dire, but the combined efforts of the United States and its allies began to have an impact. Reports from the ground indicated that Russian military operations were facing significant disruptions, and internal dissent within the Kremlin was growing as the economic and diplomatic costs of the conflict mounted.

One evening, Eleanor received an encrypted message from a high-level contact within the Russian government. The message hinted at increasing frustration and divisions among the Russian leadership, suggesting that continued pressure might force them to reconsider their aggressive stance.

Eleanor shared this information with the task force. "We might have a window of opportunity here. If we keep up the pressure and maintain our strategic approach, we could potentially force Russia back to the negotiating table."

General Whitaker and Vice President Reed agreed, emphasising the importance of maintaining a strong and unified front.

President Trent, though still visibly outraged about the situation, adhered to the agreed approach. "We will continue to put pressure on they need to understand that their actions have profound consequences."

CHAPTER SIX

RUSSIA RENEGES ON AGREEMENT

As the days turned into weeks, the relentless pressure began to yield results. The combination of military readiness, cyber disruption, economic sanctions, and diplomatic efforts gradually weakened Russia's resolve. The international community's support for Ukraine remained strong, and the Kremlin faced growing domestic and international isolation. The consensus across the international community was that 'we will support Ukraine to the end.'

Finally, under intense pressure and facing significant internal dissent, the Russian government signalled a willingness to engage in serious peace talks. President Trent, Eleanor, and the task force worked to facilitate the negotiations, aiming for a durable and enforceable agreement that would ensure the security and sovereignty of Ukraine.

In an historic summit, representatives from the US, Russia, Ukraine, EU and other key international partners gathered to negotiate the terms of peace. The talks were challenging and required delicate diplomacy, but the resolve and strategic efforts of the task force had created the conditions for progress.

After several days of intense negotiation, a new agreement was reached. Russia committed to a complete withdrawal of its forces from Ukraine, while the international community agreed to stand down its military operation in Easter Europe and agreed to a phased easing of sanctions contingent on Russia's adherence to the terms.

President Trent addressed the world, reaffirming the United States' commitment to peace and stability. "Today, we have achieved a critical step towards peace in Ukraine. This agreement is a testament to the power of strategic determination and international collaboration. We will continue to support Ukraine and ensure that this peace is maintained."

As Hitler had reneged on his agreement with the British prior to World War II and invaded Poland, so the Russians once again violated their commitments, launching missiles into Kyiv and, more dramatically into Poland. The missile strikes in Poland killed hundreds of people and destroyed critical infrastructure. Russia claimed it was an error, a malfunction of programming, but the international community was unconvinced.

The situation was dire. The violation of Polish territory, a NATO member, escalated the crisis to a new level, threatening to draw multiple nations into direct conflict.

Eleanor addressed the task force. "We are facing a crisis of unprecedented scale. The missile strikes on Poland are a direct challenge to NATO and our collective security. We need to respond with both strength and determination but avoiding direct attacks on Russian soil."

President Trent, incensed by the news, addressed the room. "This is an act of war, plain and simple. I told you diplomacy alone would not work. We cannot tolerate such blatant aggression. We must act decisively and attack Russian military and infrastructure targets." There was a silence in the room as less ardent members tried to dissuade the President from direct conflict.

General Whitaker outlined the military options. "We can further increase our military presence in Eastern Europe, deploy additional air defence systems, and restart joint military exercises with NATO forces to demonstrate our readiness. We should also consider a targeted response against Russian military assets."

Vice President Reed added, "We must rally our NATO allies and invoke Article 5. An attack on one is an attack on all. This collective defence principle is the cornerstone of our alliance. Diplomatic and economic measures should be escalated alongside our military response."

Eleanor was horrified that Reed, an ally on her team seemed to be supporting the President's demand for direct action. She spoke. "I urge caution. We need a balanced approach. To show strength but avoid direct action on Russia that could lead to an uncontrollable escalation and the use of nuclear missiles." It had become a familiar scene trying to quell the President's desire to send in the troops.

She continued "We must speak to our international partners urgently and press for a robust diplomatic and an economic crackdown but not war." As she uttered her words, she knew she had said all this before and wondered if her overtures would square with the President's frustration and anger.

As predicted, President Trent reiterated his wish to attack Russian assets in both Ukraine and on Russian territory, but something stopped him from issuing a direct order for military action. Eleanor watched the President as he paused and stumbled his words. She hoped her advice had changed his mind. "Okay. I won't issue an order for direct action, just yet, but we need to make it clear to the Russians that attacks on NATO members is a grave mistake and we will coordinate our response and build our military readiness. I will not take attacking Russian forces directly off the table, is that understood?"

Over the next 48 hours, the task force worked to implement the President's directives. US and NATO forces were mobilised, with additional troops, aircraft, and missile defence systems deployed to Poland and other Eastern European countries. Military exercises were planned to demonstrate the alliance's strength and resolve. The Polish government were encouraged not to retaliate directly and agreed it would ramp up the conflict.

Diplomatically, Eleanor led efforts to convene an emergency NATO summit. Leaders from member nations gathered to discuss the crisis and coordinate their response. President Trent delivered a powerful speech, urging unity and collective action. "We stand at a critical juncture. Our response to this aggression must be resolute and unified. Together, we can ensure the security of our nations and the principles of international law."

The NATO allies agreed to invoke Article 5, pledging mutual defence, and coordinated actions against the Russian aggression. They also announced a new round of severe economic sanctions targeting key sectors of the Russian economy, aiming to further isolate and pressure the Kremlin.

In parallel, covert operations were instigated to gather intelligence and disrupt Russian military capabilities.

Cyber units targeted Russian command and control networks, causing significant disruptions and delays in their operations.

The international community rallied around the NATO response. Condemnations of Russia's actions were swift and widespread, and offers of support came from countries around the world. The unified stance of NATO and its allies sent a powerful message to Russia: any further aggression would be met with overwhelming force and unity.

Despite the escalated situation, Eleanor knew her advice to the President had prevented the potential for a world war, at least for now. At her next meeting with President Trent, she applauded him from stepping back from the brink. "Mr President, you showed great leadership in not issuing a directive for military attacks on Russian assets that could have triggered a larger, uncontrollable conflict, or worst still, world war and the possible use of nuclear weapons. The world should thank you."

President Trent, though still deeply angered by the attacks, understood the wisdom in Eleanor's counsel and thanked her for her kind words. "We will respond with strength, but we will also keep our ultimate goal in sight: peace and security for our allies. Thank you for your kind words, Eleanor."

As the days passed, the combined military, diplomatic, and economic pressure began to take its toll on Russia. Internal dissent within the Russian government grew, and there were increasing reports of unrest and protests against the war.

In a surprising development, a high-level Russian official close to the President contacted international intermediaries, signalling a willingness to negotiate yet another ceasefire and withdraw their forces. The official cited the unsustainable economic costs and the growing internal opposition as reasons for seeking an end to the conflict. Of course, attacking a NATO member was a foolish act, deliberate or not, and the Russian President knew he was vulnerable.

Eleanor and the task force worked to facilitate the negotiations, ensuring that they were conducted under conditions that would guarantee a lasting and verifiable peace. The talks were tense and complex, but the overwhelming international pressure and the threat of further NATO action created a conducive environment for progress.

Eventually, a new agreement was reached. Russia agreed to a complete withdrawal of its forces from Ukraine and offered a half-hearted apology for attacking Poland. The international community pledged to monitor compliance. The agreement included provisions for humanitarian aid and reconstruction efforts in the affected areas funded by Russia.

President Trent once again addressed the nation and the world, reaffirming the commitment to peace and security. "Today, we have taken a significant step towards ending this crisis. This agreement is a testament to the power of unity and determination. We will continue to support our allies and uphold the principles of international law."

For the next two months, a fragile calm returned to the international stage. The successful negotiation and enforcement of the peace agreement with Russia had restored a sense of stability, albeit there was little evidence that the Russian withdrawal from Ukraine was happening at pace. However, this tentative calm was soon disrupted by unsettling news from the East.

Intelligence sources in China reported increased military activity, raising fears of an imminent invasion of Taiwan. The Chinese government had long vowed to reclaim Taiwan, asserting that it was rightfully within their territorial authority. The recent military build-up suggested that China was preparing to act on its longstanding ambition. It seemed their efforts to negotiate with the Taiwanese received outright and unequivocal rejection.

Once again, Eleanor convened an emergency meeting of the task force. "We have credible intelligence that China is preparing for a major military operation against Taiwan. This could have severe global implications and challenge our strategic interests in the Asia-Pacific region."

President Trent, visibly frustrated, responded decisively. "We cannot allow China to unilaterally alter the status quo in Taiwan. We need to send a strong message that any aggression will not be tolerated. I fear backing off from military intervention in Russia has fuelled their ambitions." It was clear the President was not about to let his team off the hook in persuading him down the diplomatic route.

General Whitaker was asked to outline the potential military options. "We should increase our naval presence in the South China Sea and as soon as practically possible conduct joint exercises with our allies in the region, including Japan, South Korea, and Australia. We must also reinforce our commitment to Taiwan's defence under the Taiwan Relations Act."

Vice President Reed added, "Diplomatically, we need to rally international support and condemn any aggressive moves by China. Economic measures, including sanctions, should be prepared to further isolate China if they proceed with their plans."

Eleanor emphasised the importance of a balanced approach. "We must show strength but also keep channels open for diplomatic dialogue. Let's use our alliances and work with regional partners to present a unified front. At the same time, we should engage with China to discourage any aggressive actions."

President Trent agreed, "Let's move forward but we will not back down we need to achieve our ambitions to de-escalate through diplomatic efforts." This was music to Eleanor's ears. The President knew the strength of the Chinese militarily and economically and knew a military intervention by the US in any form would be disastrous.

Over the next week, the United States and its allies took a series of steps to address the growing crisis. The US Navy deployed additional ships and aircraft to the region, conducting joint military exercises with Japan, South Korea, and Australia. These actions demonstrated a robust commitment to regional security.

Diplomatically, Eleanor led efforts to convene an emergency meeting of the United Nations Security Council. President Trent addressed the international community, urging a unified response to the Chinese threat against Taiwan. "We stand with Taiwan and the principles of self-determination and international law. Any attempt by China to alter the status quo through force will be met with resolute opposition."

The international community supported the US stance, with many nations expressing concern over China's military build-up and calling for restraint. Economic measures were prepared, targeting key Chinese industries and financial institutions to deter aggressive actions.

The Russians, North Korea, and Iran all wanted China to assert its authority and claim Taiwan as its own.

Behind the scenes, Eleanor and her team engaged in back-channel communications with Chinese officials, seeking to understand their intentions and dissuade them from pursuing a military solution. These efforts were delicate and required careful diplomacy to avoid escalating the situation further.

The tension continued to build. Satellite imagery and intelligence reports confirmed that China had deployed a large-scale military presence near the Taiwan Strait, heightening fears of an imminent invasion.

In a meeting with top Chinese officials, Eleanor delivered a clear and firm message. "The world is watching. Any aggressive actions against Taiwan will have severe consequences, both militarily and economically. We urge you to pursue peaceful means to address your concerns and avoid a conflict that would have catastrophic implications."

The Chinese officials, though steadfast in their claims over Taiwan, appeared to take the warnings seriously. The international pressure and the show of military strength from the US and its allies had created significant concerns.

In a surprising turn of events, China proposed renewed diplomatic talks with Taiwan under international mediation. While tensions remained high, this proposal opened a potential path to resolving the issue.

President Trent directed Eleanor and the task force to facilitate these talks. "We must ensure that these negotiations are conducted in good faith and that Taiwan's security and autonomy are upheld."

The coming weeks saw intense diplomatic efforts to bring both sides to the negotiating table. The task force worked to support the process, coordinating with international partners, and providing security guarantees to Taiwan.

While the situation remained precarious, the renewed focus on diplomacy offered a glimmer of hope. The threat of conflict had not disappeared, but the immediate danger had been averted through a combination of strength, strategic alliances, and astute diplomacy. With Russian aggression in Ukraine muted for the time being and the Middle East experiencing an unusual calm, China and its military ambitions remained the top priority of the President, until yet another flare up required US intervention.

For years undocumented immigrants entering the US from Mexico had been a hot topic and apart from the decision to 'build a wall' which in part had been achieved, the numbers of undocumented immigrants continued to multiply and preoccupied Congress. The President decided meaningful and long-lasting action was required to halt the flow and ordered US ground troops to the border with an order to shoot to kill anyone attempting to cross from midday the following Sunday. A campaign to promote the directive would be undertaken to ensure there was no misunderstanding. The US, instructed by its Commander-In-Chief, would shoot to kill anyone attempting to enter the US-Mexican border illegally.

The President's decision to deploy US ground troops to the border with orders to use lethal force against undocumented immigrants sent shockwaves through the nation and the international community. Eleanor, deeply concerned about the ethical and humanitarian implications of such a directive, sought an urgent meeting with President Trent. She was confident he had not considered the wider implications of his plan; it was another sign of his irrational behaviour.

"Mr. President, we must consider the repercussions of this order," she insisted. "This could lead to a humanitarian crisis and severe damage to our international standing. There are other ways to address border security without resorting to such extreme measures."

President Trent, though determined in his stance, acknowledged Eleanor's concerns. "I understand your apprehensions, Eleanor, but we need to demonstrate that we are serious about securing our borders. Congress and the American people demand action."

Eleanor proposed an alternative strategy, combining enhanced border security measures with increased support for legal immigration pathways and cooperation with Mexico to address the root causes of migration. "We can strengthen our border without compromising our values. Let's work with the Mexicans to create a plan that goes some way to addressing economic instability, the epidemic in illegal drug gang violence which is driving people to flee their homes. We cannot be seen to be lecturing other nations about their human rights offences and be committing our own. "

After a tense deliberation, President Trent agreed to a modified approach not believing anything other than direct action would work. She had worked her magic once again. The troops would be deployed to reinforce the border, but with strict rules of engagement that emphasised non-lethal measures and the humane treatment of migrants. In addition, a bilateral task force would be established with Mexican authorities to tackle the underlying issues of migration.

As the revised plan was implemented, Eleanor and her team coordinated with international humanitarian organisations to provide aid and legal assistance to migrants while improving the efficiency and fairness of the immigration process. The task force also launched economic development initiatives in Central America, aiming to create opportunities that would reduce the pressure for people to migrate.

The situation at the border remained complex and challenging, but Eleanor's diplomatic efforts and commitment to a balanced approach began to yield results. The number of illegal crossings decreased, and the cooperation with Mexico and Central American countries strengthened regional stability.

By advocating for a humane and comprehensive solution, she had not only prevented a potential humanitarian disaster but also upheld the nation's values and principles. The US could not contemplate undertaking such draconian measures as a 'shoot to kill' policy and simultaneously rebuke pariah states for their actions. Since the first day of meeting President Trent, Eleanor had managed to persuade him to step back from controversial and risky decision-making regarding international affairs, however, the President was becoming increasingly frustrated that his will was being manipulated.

He wanted to reassert his authority and to reset the relationship with his team. His message was forthright. 'I am Commander-in-Chief, and my orders should be carried out without challenge.' The President summoned Eleanor to his office.

As Eleanor made her way to the Oval Office, she felt uneasy. President Trent's summons had come unexpectedly, and she could sense that a confrontation was imminent. She took a deep breath, steeling herself for the conversation ahead.

Entering the room, she saw the President standing by his desk, his expression stern. He motioned for her to sit down, she did so.

" Eleanor. I've been reflecting on our working relationship and the recent decisions we've made. While I appreciate your counsel, it's become clear to me that I need to reassert my authority as Commander-in-Chief. I have been continually undermined. I am the elected leader of this nation, and my orders should be carried out without hesitation or challenge."

Eleanor understood the mind of the President, and the reason for his frustration. He wanted control without debate, believing he knew best; advisers were there to implement his orders not seek to persuade him to their way of thinking. It was stereotypical of his psychopathic tendencies. "Mr. President, I respect your position and the immense responsibilities that come with it. My role has always been to support and advise you to the best of my abilities, ensuring that our decisions are well-informed and in the best interest of the nation."

President Trent leaned forward. "I understand that, Eleanor. But there have been many occasions when my decisions were overruled or side-stepped. This must change. From now on, I expect my directives to be followed without question."

Eleanor met his gaze, her voice steady. "I hear you, Mr. President. However, I must emphasise the importance of a collaborative approach, especially when it comes to matters of national and international security. Your advisers, including myself, are here to provide you with the best possible guidance. That said, I will respect your directive and ensure that our team aligns more closely with your leadership."

President Trent's expression softened slightly. "I appreciate your understanding, Eleanor. It's crucial that we present a united front, both to our allies and adversaries. We must show strength and decisiveness, but I won't be a puppet manipulated by my closest advisers."

Eleanor nodded. "I understand, sir. I hope together we can arrive at accommodations in the future over key issues that satisfies you as President and the needs of the country." This was Eleanor's diplomatic way of saying 'You won't have free reign.

The President seemed satisfied with her response not fully absorbing what she had said. "Good. Let's move forward with a renewed sense of purpose and unity. There are significant challenges ahead, and we need to be prepared to face them."

As Eleanor left the Oval Office, she reflected on the conversation. It was clear that the President was determined to assert his authority, and she would need to navigate her future discussions with him carefully.

Eleanor gathered her trusted advisers in the secure conference room within the White House. As they settled in, she could see the concern in their eyes, mirroring her own apprehensions. The room was filled with key figures from various departments, all integral to navigating the delicate political landscape they were facing.

"Thank you all for coming on such short notice," Eleanor began, her tone serious but calm. "I wanted to share with you the outcome of my meeting with President Trent and provide some context to help us move forward effectively."

She paused, gathering her thoughts. "President Trent expressed his frustration with what he perceives as a lack of adherence to his directives. He emphasised that he expects his orders to be executed without question. This is a significant shift in our dynamic and one we need to manage with utmost care."

The room remained silent as Eleanor continued. "As some of you know, I have a background in psychiatry, and I believe it's important to understand the psychological aspects of leadership and decision-making, especially under the immense pressures of the presidency."

She made eye contact with each member of her team. "The President's need to reassert his authority is not uncommon in high-stress roles, particularly when feeling undermined or challenged. This can sometimes lead to more impulsive or rigid decision-making, driven by a desire to maintain control. It's crucial that we work around this carefully to avoid potential pitfalls."

One of the advisers, a seasoned diplomat, spoke up. "Eleanor, what specific dangers do you foresee if we don't adapt to this new situation?"

Eleanor responded "The main danger is the potential for unilateral decisions that may not fully consider the wider implications. This can lead to international incidents, economic repercussions, or even unnecessary military conflicts. Our role is to ensure that we continue to provide the best possible advice while respecting the President's directives. It's a delicate balance, but one we must achieve." A national security expert, nodded in agreement. "We need to be careful in how we present information and recommendations. Perhaps framing our advice in a way that aligns more closely with his vision and emphasising the benefits of collaborative decision-making."

Eleanor smiled slightly, appreciating the input. "Exactly. We need to support the President while gently steering decisions toward the most beneficial outcomes. It will require tact, diplomacy, and a unified approach from all of us."

She concluded the meeting. "Let's stay focused and work together closely. Our priority remains the security and well-being of the nation. If we can navigate this with skill and care, we can continue to guide our country through these challenging times."

Eleanor knew it would be difficult managing President Trent's leadership and in doing so safeguard the nation's future. She knew she was now playing a pivotal role within the Administration and that came with huge responsibility.

CHAPTER SEVEN

US-MEXICAN BORDER CRISIS

Soon after Eleanor's briefing, the President summoned his military team to the Oval Office but deliberately excluded Eleanor from the invitation list, he was beginning to work out that she had been a leading force behind the manipulation of his past decision-making and wanted to assess his other advisers.

The Oval Office filled with key military leaders and national security officials, all keenly aware of the President's recent declaration to reassert his command.

As they settled in, President Trent wasted no time getting to the point. "Thank you all for coming. I have made it clear that as Commander-in-Chief my directives must be followed without question. Today, I want to discuss our current military posture and strategy, particularly concerning China, Taiwan, and the situation at the southern border."

General Robert Harris, a seasoned and respected figure in the military, spoke first. "Mr. President, we are of course prepared to follow your directives. Our forces are ready to respond to any threats, and we continue to monitor the situation in the Taiwan Strait closely, and our presence in the region remains strong."

President Trent nodded, appreciating the direct response. "What about the border? I've ordered troops to be stationed there with strict rules of engagement. How is that progressing?"

General Harris replied, "The troops have been deployed as per your orders. We've implemented strict protocols to ensure the security of the border while minimising unnecessary force. Our goal is to uphold your directive while maintaining humanitarian considerations."

President Trent's expression hardened slightly. "I want to ensure that my orders are being executed without dilution.

We cannot afford to show weakness, especially with the ongoing immigration crisis. Are there any concerns or objections from the rest of you?"

Admiral Susan Lee, another senior member of the military team, hesitated for a moment before speaking. "Mr. President, while we fully support your authority and leadership, it's important to consider the long-term implications of our actions. Strict rules of engagement at the border need to be balanced with humanitarian considerations to avoid potential backlash both domestically and internationally."

President Trent's eyes narrowed. "Are you suggesting that my orders are not in the best interest of the country?"

Admiral Lee met his gaze steadily. "Not at all, Mr. President. I am merely suggesting that we approach this with a comprehensive strategy that includes security, diplomacy, and humanitarian aspects. This will strengthen our position and uphold our values."

The President paused, considering her words. It was clear he was testing the loyalty and judgment of his military advisers. "I appreciate your input, Admiral. It's crucial that we present a united front. However, I expect my orders to be executed as given. We need to show strength and decisiveness."

He turned to the rest of the team. "Is there anyone else who has concerns about following my directives?"

The room remained silent the tension palpable. The military leaders understood the delicate balance they needed to maintain between supporting the President's authority and providing their professional judgement.

President Trent concluded the meeting with a firm tone. "Very well. Ensure that our military posture remains strong and that my orders are carried out. We must demonstrate our resolve to both our allies and adversaries. "

As the military team departed, the President felt a mixture of satisfaction and unease. He had asserted his authority, but the subtle reluctance from some of his advisers hinted at the ongoing complexity of his leadership.

Meanwhile, Eleanor, aware of the meeting but not its details, continued work in her office expecting to be briefed later. She understood her role as a Special Adviser was under threat if she failed to meet the President's expectations. The challenges ahead were formidable, but she remained optimistic she could play a pivotal role in saving the country from its psychopathic President.

News that the Mexican border crisis had deteriorated, and a substantial number of undocumented immigrants captured were known drug and people smugglers, infuriated President Trent. He summoned, once again, his senior advisers and key military leaders to the Oval Office for an emergency meeting. This time, Eleanor was included indicating that the President was ready to confront her directly.

President Trent stood at his desk, a copy of the report in his hand which he tossed to the floor. "This is unacceptable," he began, his voice rich with anger. "I ordered strict measures be adopted at the border, yet the situation has got worse. This report shows that our borders are not secure and that seriously dangerous individuals are exploiting our weaknesses. I want immediate action."

Eleanor spoke up, knowing this may be her last speech before being fired. "Mr. President, while the situation has deteriorated in the numbers of people attempting to cross the border, we have arrested a record number of people that have be detained, and in some cases will be incarcerated for their crimes. I guarantee from the intelligence I have seen that the numbers crossing will decline in the weeks and months ahead as our new regime of border surveillance and control begins to bite…" She paused fearful of the President's reaction to the next few words she would utter. "…We have enacted your orders except for a 'shoot to kill' policy, that if pursued, would guarantee the destruction of our credibility as the world's leading democracy that upholds the rule of law, and destroy your Presidential legacy. You would be tarnished with the same brush that paints the leaders of our adversaries as evil dictators."

There was silence in the room. All eyes were on Eleanor. She retained her composure and looked the President squarely in the eyes.

President Trent stared at Eleanor trying to fathom a suitable response.

He failed to say anything to her and pressed on directing his comments at the rest of the assembled group. "I'm sorry this is not the time for caution. We need decisive action. Our current measures are clearly insufficient. General Harris, what are our options?"

General Harris, who had been closely monitoring the situation, stepped forward. "Mr. President, we can increase the military presence still further at the border and implement more aggressive interception strategies. However, we must also consider the legal and ethical implications of such actions. Using excessive force could lead to civilian casualties and, as Eleanor has said damage our international reputation." Siding with Eleanor was a risky strategy for the General who the President saw as a supporter of his hard-line policies.

The President clenched his jaw, visibly frustrated. "I am tired of hearing about implications. We need results. Admiral Lee, what do you propose?"

Admiral Lee responded, "Mr. President, while increasing our border security is crucial, we should also ramp up our discussions with the Mexican authorities to dismantle the smuggling networks. A collaborative approach could yield better long-term results and mitigate some of the risks associated with a purely militaristic response, but it takes time." She too was challenging the President's wishes.

The President's frustration was evident. "I want immediate action. Eleanor, you have always said the same thing, emphasising a balanced approach using what I consider flowery language, but it has achieved nothing. What makes you think the new regime at the border will significantly reduce numbers in the months ahead?"

Eleanor knew the delicacy of the situation. The President's question indicated he was retreating from his hard-line policies once more. She had always monitored his facial expressions and language to better understand what was going on in his mind. It could be threatening draconian measures to deal with complex issues was his way of appearing to assert his authority, but with little expectation they would be conducted. Accepting that scenario was a risk she was not prepared to take.

"Mr. President, we should install advanced surveillance technology and increased patrols. Simultaneously, we must put severe pressure on the Mexican government to target the smuggling networks at their source. Failure to comply would result in economic and trade sanction they have never experienced before. Additionally, we should expedite the processing of legal immigrants to reduce the pressure at the border."

She continued, "Furthermore, we need a public communication strategy to explain our actions and emphasise our commitment to both security and humanitarian values. This will help mitigate potential backlash and maintain public support."

President Trent liked her more assertive tone. He looked around the room, weighing the input of his advisers. "Very well. We will implement a dual strategy: increasing our border security measures immediately while engaging with Mexican authorities to address the root causes. General Harris, I want a detailed plan for enhanced border security on my desk by tomorrow morning. Admiral Lee, begin coordinating with Mexican officials immediately. If you all fail with your promises I will act. I hope that's clear."

He turned to Eleanor. "And Eleanor, I want you to oversee the communication strategy and ensure that our actions are effectively conveyed to the public. This crisis needs to be managed swiftly and decisively. People need to know if all fails, I will act with all the force necessary."

As the meeting concluded, Eleanor knew the options open to her and her team to keep the President from conducting his threats were narrowing.

The mounting pressure from the House over the immigration report added to President Trent's frustration. Despite his desire for more stringent action, once again his advisers had persuaded him to take a more measured approach. Feeling cornered and eager to assert his authority, the President decided to call a press conference to address the nation and outline his plan for dealing with the crisis.

As the time for the press conference approached, Eleanor and her inner circle prepared to support the President, aware of the delicate balance they needed to maintain.

They knew that the President was feeling undermined, and that their role was to provide the best possible advice while respecting his authority.

Standing at the podium, President Trent looked poised and in control. The room was filled with journalists, their eyes trained on him, ready to capture every word.

"My fellow Americans," he began, "The recent immigration report has highlighted a serious and ongoing issue at our southern border. I want to assure you that I share the concerns of our citizens and members of Congress. Our borders must be secure, and we must prevent dangerous individuals from entering our country."

He paused, allowing his words to sink in. "In light of the recent developments, I am directing the following immediate actions: First, we will significantly increase the military presence at the border. This will include additional troops, advanced surveillance technology, and enhanced patrols. Our goal is to ensure that our borders are secure and that those who attempt to cross illegally are intercepted swiftly."

The President continued, "Second, we will intensify our collaboration with the Mexican authorities to dismantle the smuggling networks that facilitate illegal immigration and criminal activities. This will involve coordinated operations and intelligence sharing to target these organisations at their source. This is not a new initiative, but we are confident ramping up our policy will deliver measurable results in the months ahead." Eleanor's words to the President had resonated and as she listened, she hoped her analysis was right. Time would tell.

He looked directly into the cameras his expression serious. "Third, we will accelerate the processing of legal immigrants to reduce the pressure at the border. This includes increasing resources for immigration services to ensure that those who seek to enter our country legally are given the opportunity to do so in a timely manner and according to our rules."

President Trent's tone softened slightly as he addressed the humanitarian aspect. "While we must be firm in our approach, we will also uphold our values and ensure that our actions are humane. Our commitment to security does not diminish our responsibility to treat all individuals with dignity and respect."

Concluding his address, he said, "I want to assure the American people that we are taking decisive action to address this crisis. We will protect our borders, uphold our laws, and ensure the safety and security of our nation. It will take time, but I am confident we will win this war."

After the press conference, President Trent returned to the Oval Office, where Eleanor and the rest of his senior advisers were waiting. He seemed more composed but still determined to see his directives implemented without further delay.

" I appreciate everyone's counsel, but it's clear to me at least that stronger action is needed if we are to control illegal immigration. I expect your full support in executing the measures we've agreed," he said, his tone leaving no room for disagreement.

Eleanor smiled awkwardly understanding the gravity of the situation. "You have our full support, Mr. President.

As the team dispersed to implement the President's orders, Eleanor reflected on the day's events. The President had made his stance clear, and the path forward would require careful navigation to balance security, diplomacy, and humanitarian concerns. She remained committed to her contribution in guiding the nation through this challenging time, knowing that the stakes were higher than ever.

In the days following the President's press conference, the White House was a hive of activity. The President's directives were being put into action with urgency, and every department was working at full capacity to ensure the success of the new strategy.

Eleanor called another meeting with her inner circle to make sure all aspects of the plan had been covered off. She understood that the increased military presence and the collaboration with Mexican authorities needed to be managed meticulously to avoid potential clangers.

"Thank you all for coming," Eleanor began. "As you know, the President has made his stance clear, and we all should be proud that he has listened to our advice and stepped back from draconian measures that could have spectacularly backfired." Several people smiled and nodded agreeing with her analysis.

She continued. "It's our job to ensure his directives are executed efficiently and effectively. Let's go over the key areas and address any concerns or potential issues."

General Harris, who had been leading the military efforts at the border, provided an update. "We've deployed additional troops and advanced surveillance technology will be installed in the next few weeks. Our enhanced patrols have already resulted in a significant increase in interceptions. However, we need to be cautious about the rules of engagement to avoid unnecessary violence and potential human rights violations."

Eleanor nodded. "Absolutely. We must strike a balance between security and humanitarian considerations. Admiral Lee, how are the talks with Mexican authorities progressing?"

Admiral Lee responded, "We've established a task force with Mexican officials, focusing on intelligence sharing and coordinated operations but a meeting date is yet to be agreed. Already there's been some initial success in targeting smuggling networks, but it's clear that this will be a long-term effort. We need to ensure sustained cooperation and support from the Mexican government."

Eleanor turned to the immigration services representative. "What about the plan for processing legal immigrants?"

The representative replied, "We've increased resources and discussed streamlining processes, which in time will reduced wait times but it won't happen overnight. The volume of applications is at its highest, and we will need additional resources to maintain pace, but everything is in hand."

Eleanor made a few notes before addressing the group again. "It's crucial that we maintain transparency and keep the public informed about our efforts. We need to communicate the positive impacts of our actions and ensure that the President's message is clearly conveyed."

The communications director added, "We're planning a series of briefings and updates to keep the public informed. We'll highlight the increased security at the border and our collaborative efforts with Mexico.

We'll also emphasise the expedited processing regime for legal immigrants to show that we're addressing the issue comprehensively."

Eleanor concluded the meeting with a sense of accomplishment. "Thank you, everyone. Let's keep up the good work and stay focused. The President is counting on us to deliver results, and the nation's security and well-being depend on our success."

The President's frustration and the pressure from Congress were clear indicators of the high stakes involved. Eleanor knew the coming months would be challenging and the President would be looking for results.

.

CHAPTER EIGHT

SCHOOL SHOOTINGS SHOCK THE NATION

In the following weeks, the situation at the border showed signs of improvement. The increased military presence and advanced surveillance technology significantly reduced illegal crossings. The collaboration with Mexican authorities led to the dismantling of several smuggling networks, and the expedited processing of legal immigrants alleviated some of the pressure.

Eleanor understood that the underlying issues driving migration were complex and not confined to Mexico and Mexican's alone trying to cross the border. At least forty percent of illegal crossings were people escaping regimes in South America. The President's modified decisions had brought temporary relief, but the long-term solution required addressing the root causes of migration and maintaining a balance between security and humanitarian values.

The atmosphere in the White House was tense as President Trent and his senior advisers grappled with a series of domestic crises. The violence in Detroit and the tragic school shooting in Ohio had shocked the nation, intensifying the pressure on the President to take decisive action on gun reform and public safety. The President knew that his response would be scrutinised closely by both the public and his political opponents.

President Trent called an emergency meeting with his inner circle, including Eleanor, to address the mounting domestic issues. As they gathered in the Situation Room, the weight of recent events was evident.

"Thank you for coming on such short notice," the President began. "The events in Detroit and Ohio are tragedies that cannot be ignored. We need to address these issues head-on and provide the American people with clear solutions."

Eleanor spoke first, understanding the urgency of the situation. "Mr. President, we must address the immediate need for peace and security in Detroit.

This requires a coordinated response between law enforcement, community leaders, and social services to prevent further violence and restore order."

The Secretary of Homeland Security added, "We are already collaborating with local authorities in Detroit to de-escalate tensions and provide support. However, we need to ensure that this is not a temporary fix. Long-term investment in the community and police reform is essential to prevent future clashes."

The President nodded, then turned his attention to the school shooting in Ohio. "The shooting in Ohio is a stark reminder of the urgent need for gun reform. We cannot continue to allow these tragedies to occur. We need to take bold action to protect our children and communities."

Eleanor spoke, "Mr. President, we must push for comprehensive gun reform legislation. This includes universal background checks, banning assault weapons, and implementing stricter regulations on gun ownership. We need to work with Congress to build bipartisan support for these measures. I know this topic has raised its head on many occasions over the decades but under your Presidency we have an opportunity to make progress, a top-down review of the pros and cons of reform. We must get Congress on board and that won't be easy."

The Vice President, a key ally in the administration, added, "We should also consider executive actions that can be taken immediately to address gun violence. This includes strengthening enforcement of existing laws and increasing funding for mental health services and school safety programmes."

President Trent looked around the room, his expression determined. "I want an outline plan on my desk by the end of the week. We need immediate actions and long-term strategies. We will address the violence in Detroit and push forward with gun reform. The American people need to see that we are taking these issues seriously."

As the meeting adjourned, Eleanor and her team set to work. They began drafting a comprehensive plan that addressed both the immediate and systemic issues contributing to the recent tragedies.

Over time, the administration rolled out a series of initiatives aimed at restoring peace in Detroit and advancing gun reform. The President announced increased federal support for community programmes, alongside efforts to foster dialogue between police and residents. Additionally, a task force was established to investigate the root causes of the violence and recommend long-term solutions. Bringing about change would not be easy.

On the gun reform front, the President held a series of high-profile meetings with lawmakers from both parties, advocating for comprehensive legislation. He also signed several executive orders aimed at strengthening background checks and increasing funding for mental health services and school security. Gun reform had always been a hot topic and change of any kind had been vehemently opposed by lobby groups and senators financed by firearm manufacturers and specifically the National Rifle Association.

The President addressed the nation from the Oval Office. "These tragedies in Detroit and Ohio remind us of the urgent need for change. We must come together as a nation to address the root causes of violence and take meaningful steps to ensure the safety of our communities. My administration is committed to pursuing comprehensive solutions that protect our citizens and uphold our values." It was a hollow statement, for he knew the possession of firearms in the US was a right enshrined in the constitution, and reforming the constitution to remove guns from the streets would never happen. Gun ownership would rise significantly in the years to come irrespective of the measures any President was prepared to undertake.

The response from the public and media was mixed, as it always was regarding this topic. While many praised the President for his decisive action and commitment to gun reform, others criticised the measures as insufficient and politically motivated.

The recent events had underscored the importance of addressing both domestic and international issues with the same level of urgency and determination. There was no respite.

In the weeks following the President's address to the nation, the administration's efforts to tackle the domestic crises began to take shape.

The multi-faceted approach outlined by Eleanor and the inner circle was put into action.

In Detroit, the federal government launched a comprehensive support initiative. Eleanor, working closely with the Secretary of Homeland Security and the Attorney General, ensured that resources were directed toward both immediate peacekeeping and long-term community rebuilding efforts.

A federal task force was despatched to work with local law enforcement, community leaders, and social service agencies. Their plan was to de-escalate tensions, provide conflict resolution training, and establish a platform for continuous dialogue between police and residents. The task force also aimed to implement police reform measures that included better training, accountability, and community policing practices.

Eleanor frequently visited Detroit to oversee the efforts and meet with stakeholders. In one of her town hall meetings, she emphasised, "This is not just about restoring order but about building trust and creating sustainable peace. We are committed to ensuring that all citizens feel safe and respected."

The efforts began to show signs of progress. There was a noticeable reduction in violence, and community programs started to gain traction. However, Eleanor knew that real change would take time and consistent effort beyond one or two presidential terms. Meanwhile, the push for gun reform faced significant resistance in Congress. Despite the public outcry following the Ohio school shooting, several lawmakers remained staunchly opposed to any changes in gun laws. The administration had to navigate a deeply polarised political landscape.

President Trent, with Eleanor's counsel persisted initiating a bipartisan effort to garner support for reform. He met privately with key senators and representatives, trying to bridge the divide. Eleanor facilitated these discussions, often using her diplomatic skills to find common ground.

To increase public pressure, the administration launched a nationwide campaign, involving survivors of gun violence, law enforcement officials, and educators. Town hall meetings, public rallies, and media appearances were organised to highlight the urgent need for change.

The stories of those affected by gun violence resonated deeply with the public, creating a groundswell of support.

Despite the hurdles, President Trent moved forward with several executive actions. He signed orders to strengthen background checks and allocate additional funding for mental health services and school security. These actions were designed to make immediate impacts while the legislative battle continued.

Simultaneously, the administration worked to draft a comprehensive gun reform bill. The proposed legislation included universal background checks, a ban on assault weapons, and measures to address illegal gun trafficking.

As the bill was introduced in Congress, Eleanor and her team prepared for an intense lobbying effort. They met with undecided lawmakers, presented compelling data and personal testimonies, and built coalitions with advocacy groups. The pressure was mounting, but so was the momentum for change.

The culmination of these efforts came during a critical vote in the House of Representatives. The chamber was packed, with every lawmaker present knowing the significance of their decision. President Trent and Eleanor watched anxiously from the Oval Office as the votes were counted.

After a tense period, the bill passed with the narrowest of margins. The news was met with a mix of relief and celebration within the White House. Eleanor allowed herself a moment of satisfaction before refocusing on the next steps. The Senate vote loomed ahead, and the fight was far from over.

In a reflective moment with her inner circle, Eleanor emphasised, "We've made significant strides, but we cannot become complacent. Our work is ongoing, and we must continue to push forward, guided by our principles and the needs of the people."

As the administration moved into the next phase of its agenda, Eleanor remained a pivotal figure, guiding the President through the complexities of governance.

The challenges were immense, but with determination, strategic thinking, and the support of a dedicated team, she was confident they could achieve lasting positive change for the nation.

A state visit to the UK approached, the atmosphere in the White House was a mix of relief and apprehension. The senior advisers, including Eleanor, were meticulously planning every detail to ensure the trip went smoothly. The visit presented an opportunity for President Trent to strengthen international relations and highlight his diplomatic skills, but it also carried the risk of potential errors of judgement on a global stage.

In the days leading up to the departure, Eleanor held several meetings with the President and his team to go over the itinerary and key talking points. She understood the importance of presenting a unified and composed image during the visit, especially given the domestic challenges the administration was facing.

"Mr. President, this visit is a significant opportunity to reinforce our relationship with the UK and to highlight our shared values and goals," Eleanor began in one of the briefings. "Your speech to the British Parliament will be a centrepiece of the trip. It's crucial that we strike the right tone, emphasising unity, cooperation, and mutual respect."

The communications director added, "We've prepared a draft of your speech, focusing on key themes such as the special relationship between our countries, the importance of NATO, and our commitment to global security and economic stability. We've also included some personal anecdotes to make the speech more relatable." President Trent reviewed the speech, nodding thoughtfully.

Despite the thorough preparations, Eleanor knew that the President tended to speak off-the-cuff, which sometimes led to unintended consequences. To mitigate this risk, she arranged for additional rehearsals and briefings on the cultural and political nuances of the UK.

"Mr. President," she advised during one of the rehearsals, "While it's important to be genuine and engaging, please remember to stick to the prepared remarks during your speech and official meetings. Any ad-libbed comments should be carefully considered to avoid misunderstandings."

The President smiled wryly. "I'll do my best, Eleanor. I know this trip is important."

On the day of the departure, Air Force One was a hub of activity. Eleanor and the senior advisers used the flight time to go over final details and ensure the President was fully briefed on all aspects of the visit. They discussed potential questions from the press, the protocol for meeting King Charles III, and the topics likely to come up during discussions with British officials.

"Remember, Mr. President, King Charles is deeply invested in environmental issues," Eleanor noted. "It would be beneficial to acknowledge his efforts and express our administration's commitment to tackling climate change."

Upon landing in London, the President and his entourage were greeted with a formal ceremony. Eleanor watched closely, noting the warm reception and the meticulous attention to protocol. The President appeared composed and confident, which was reassuring.

The first day of the visit went smoothly, with President Trent engaging in meetings with the British Prime Minister and other key officials. Eleanor made sure to always be present, ready to provide support and guidance as needed.

The highlight of the visit was the President's speech to the British Parliament. The historic setting and the presence of dignitaries and lawmakers added to the gravity of the moment. As President Trent stepped up to the podium, Eleanor felt a mixture of pride and nervousness.

The President began his speech, and Eleanor listened intently. He spoke eloquently about the enduring alliance between the United States and the United Kingdom, the shared history and values, and the joint efforts to promote peace and prosperity. He praised King Charles III's environmental advocacy and reaffirmed the commitment to tackling climate change.

"The special relationship between our nations is built on a foundation of mutual respect, trust, and common goals," the President declared.

"Together, we face global challenges with determination and unity, knowing that our strength lies in our partnership."

As the speech concluded to a standing ovation, Eleanor allowed herself a moment of relief. The President had delivered his remarks flawlessly, and the positive response from the British Parliament was a testament to the effectiveness of their preparation.

The remainder of the visit included a state dinner with King Charles III, where the President and the King engaged in thoughtful discussion about environmental issues, international relations, and the future of the transatlantic alliance. Eleanor observed that the President handled himself with grace and diplomacy, further solidifying the success of the trip.

On the flight back to the United States, the mood on Air Force One was markedly lighter. The state visit had been a triumph, and the President's team was pleased with the positive coverage and the strengthening of US-UK relations.

"Well done, Mr. President," Eleanor said, offering a genuine smile. "This visit has been a significant success. Your speech was well-received, and we've reinforced our relationship with one of our closest allies."

President Trent nodded, visibly relieved. "Thank you, Eleanor. I couldn't have done it without all your support. Now, let's focus on addressing the challenges we have at home with the same determination."

As the White House settled into a normal routine with the President in the Oval Office, news came in that a major riot had broken out in Chicago after a period of public frustration over welfare reform and unemployment. Politically, the President had to intervene.

Eleanor quickly gathered the senior staff for an emergency meeting. The atmosphere was tense as they reviewed the reports coming in from Chicago. The images of burning buildings, clashes between protestors and police, and the palpable anger of local people filled the room with a sense of urgency.

"We need to act swiftly," the President said. "We cannot let this situation spiral out of control."

"Mr. President, we should consider a televised address," Eleanor suggested. "The people need to hear from you directly. We need to show that you are aware of their frustrations and are committed to addressing their concerns."

"Agreed," the President replied. "But we also need to deploy resources to restore order and provide immediate relief."

The Chief of Staff outlined a plan: the National Guard would be mobilised to assist local law enforcement, and the Federal Emergency Management Agency – FEMA- would be dispatched to provide aid to those affected by the violence. Additionally, the President would hold a press conference to announce a task force dedicated to reviewing welfare policies and unemployment solutions.

Within hours, the President was standing in front of the cameras, addressing the nation. "My fellow Americans, today we face a grave situation in Chicago. The frustrations of our people are both seen and heard, and we need to do more to address the challenges they face. Effective immediately, I am deploying the National Guard to assist in restoring peace and ensuring the safety of all residents.

Furthermore, I am establishing a task force to review our welfare and unemployment policies, with a commitment to finding real solutions that will benefit all Americans. We must work together to build a future where everyone can succeed. Let us come together in this moment of crisis, not as adversaries, but as one nation, determined to overcome our difficulties and build a better tomorrow."

The President's words were well received with some praising his swift action and empathetic tone, others remained sceptical, demanding concrete changes rather than promises.

In the following days, Eleanor and the President worked with the newly formed task force, meeting with community leaders, economists, and social workers to develop comprehensive reform proposals. The administration also focused on improving communication and transparency with the public, aiming to rebuild trust and demonstrate their commitment to meaningful change.

As the initial chaos in Chicago began to subside, Eleanor knew that this was only the beginning. The challenges at home were immense. Chicago was not the only hotspot in the country; riots had broken out in more than a dozen cities, due to a cost-of-living crisis, the need for welfare reform, and high unemployment. It was clear the government had little headroom to resolve everyone's demands and needed to take firm action to stabilise the situation. COVID funding had taken its toll on government finances, and the government deficit was spiralling out of control.

The following morning, the President convened an emergency meeting with key members of his Cabinet, senior advisers, and representatives from the National Guard and Homeland Security. The gravity of the situation was evident as reports of escalating violence and unrest poured in from across the nation.

"We're facing a nationwide crisis," the President began. "We need a plan that addresses both the immediate need for order and the underlying issues driving these riots."

The Secretary of Defence outlined a plan to deploy the National Guard to affected cities, working in conjunction with local law enforcement to restore order and protect lives and property. The Secretary of Health and Human Services proposed immediate emergency relief measures, including food aid and temporary housing assistance for those most affected by the economic crisis.

Eleanor, recognising the need for both immediate action and long-term solutions, suggested a two-pronged approach: "Mr. President, we need to stabilise the situation on the ground first, but we also need to show the public that we are committed to real, substantive changes. We should announce a comprehensive economic recovery plan that addresses the root causes of these riots."

The President nodded in agreement. "Let's move forward with both tracks. We'll deploy the National Guard to restore order and provide immediate relief, and we'll also announce a national economic recovery initiative focused on job creation, affordable housing, and welfare reform." By noon, the President addressed the nation from the Oval Office.

"My fellow Americans, we are facing a homeland crisis. The riots we are witnessing in cities across our nation are a clear indication of the deep frustration and suffering felt by many. Primarily, we must restore peace and ensure the safety of all citizens. I have authorised the deployment of the National Guard to support local law enforcement in maintaining order and protecting our communities. At the same time, we must address the underlying issues that have led to this unrest. Today, I am announcing a comprehensive national economic recovery initiative. This plan includes significant investments in job creation programmes, expansion of affordable housing, and a thorough review and reform of our welfare system to ensure it meets the needs of our citizens. We are committed to listening to your concerns and working to create a fair and just society where everyone can thrive. Let us come together in this moment of crisis, united by our shared determination to build a better future for all."

In the days that followed, the administration worked to implement the President's plan. National Guard units were deployed to restore order in riot-stricken areas, simultaneously, the task force began drafting detailed proposals for job creation, housing, and welfare reform.

Eleanor coordinated with community leaders, economists, and social workers to ensure the administration's policies were informed by a diverse range of perspectives and expertise. The President held town hall meetings and listening sessions to engage directly with the public and rebuild trust.

The situation remained tense, but the administration's decisive actions and commitment to meaningful change gradually began to restore a sense of stability.

Eleanor and the President's senior advisers gathered to discuss the next phase of their strategy. It was clear that long-term solutions were needed to stabilise the country and rebuild trust between the government and the people.

"Mr. President," Eleanor began, "we need to show that we're not just reacting to this crisis, but that we're committed to a sustained effort to improve the lives of our citizens. We should expand our economic recovery initiative to include comprehensive education reform, healthcare improvements, and targeted support for small businesses."

The President nodded. "We need a New Deal for the modern era. Let's outline a detailed plan and present it to Congress immediately. We also need to engage directly with the communities most affected by these issues."

The administration prepared what was termed 'The Modern New Deal' a sweeping set of proposals aimed at addressing the systemic issues that had led to the current unrest.

The President presented the Modern New Deal to Congress, urging swift bipartisan action. Meanwhile, he and Eleanor travelled to several of the cities most affected by the riots to hold town hall meetings and listening sessions. They met with local leaders, activists, and ordinary people to hear their concerns and gather input on the proposed initiatives.

In one of these meetings in Detroit, a young single mother named Maria spoke passionately about the struggles she faced trying to provide for her children on a minimum-wage job with limited access to affordable childcare and healthcare.

"Mr. President," Maria said, her voice trembling, "We need more than just promises. We need real, tangible help. My kids deserve a future where they can have a decent life, not just survive."

The President listened intently, moved by Maria's words. "Maria, I hear you, and I promise that we are committed to making real changes. We won't rest until every American can build a better life for themselves and their families."

As the administration pushed forward with the Modern New Deal, they faced significant opposition from some lawmakers and interest groups. However, the public support for the initiative was strong, driven by the administration's transparency and engagement with the communities most affected.

The media coverage began to shift, highlighting the administration's efforts and the positive impact of the immediate relief measures. Stories emerged of families receiving much-needed aid, small businesses starting to recover, and communities coming together to rebuild.

Eleanor knew there was still much work to be done, but the progress they were making provided a glimmer of hope. The President's decisive action and commitment to a comprehensive, long-term solution were beginning to restore stability and trust.

CHAPTER NINE

HURRICANS DEVASTATE GULF OF MEXICO

The White House was braced, the early start of the hurricane season implied trouble. Forecasts showed erratic jet stream patterns, predicting a relentless series of high-intensity hurricanes that would tear through the Caribbean and into the Gulf of Mexico. New Orleans, still reeling from previous disasters, had seen tens of billions of dollars invested in defence systems and infrastructure rebuilding by Presidential order. In tests, it was shown that only some of the new installation would be effective against category four hurricanes, the remained woefully inadequate as construction had proved more difficult than first planned and budgets had been cut.

The first hurricane of the season, named Martha, formed in the Caribbean Sea and was on a collision course with Florida. Analysts were deeply concerned, as predictions placed Martha at a category four with winds ranging between 130mph and 156mph. Such a storm threatened catastrophic damage and inevitable loss of life if it were to hit Florida's coast. Evacuation orders went out to the coastal population, but time was against them.

As Martha gained strength, it was upgraded to a category five. The White House and Homeland Security knew that any further orders would come too late, and the storm's consequences would be far more severe than anticipated. When Martha made land, Miami bore the brunt first, followed by a path of destruction that stretched from New Orleans to Galveston. Thousands of homes were obliterated, industries were decimated, and utilities were torn apart.

As Hurricane Martha tore through Miami, the scenes of chaos and destruction were broadcast live, shaking the entire nation. Buildings crumbled and were washed away, streets flooded in some instances to depths of twelve feet, and trees were uprooted and tossed into the air like wooden lolly sticks.

Emergency services were overwhelmed, struggling to respond to countless distress calls. Hospitals braced for a surge in casualties, setting up makeshift triage centres to manage the influx. It was chaotic to say the least.

The situation in New Orleans was eerily reminiscent of past hurricanes, but this time, the new defence systems were put to the test. Levees and flood barriers, reinforced and newly constructed, held firm in many places, reducing the extent of flooding compared to previous disasters. However, the sheer power of Martha overwhelmed more vulnerable areas, leading to severe damage and loss of property. The city's residents, many of whom had experienced such devastation before, faced the storm with a mixture of dread and resilience.

Galveston, too, faced the wrath of Martha. The coastal city's industries, especially its vital shipping and oil sectors, suffered massive hits. Oil rigs and refineries were shut down as precautionary measures, but many sustained damages, leading to concerns about environmental impacts and economic repercussions. The ripple effects were felt nationwide, with fuel prices rising rapidly and supply chains disrupted.

In the days following the hurricane, the scale of the disaster became apparent. Entire neighbourhoods were reduced to rubble, and power outages were widespread. Utility companies worked tirelessly to restore electricity, but the damage to the grid meant it would be weeks before some areas saw power again. Water supplies were contaminated.

FEMA and other federal agencies mobilised quickly, setting up disaster response centres coordinating with state and local authorities. The National Guard was deployed to assist with search and rescue operations, delivering supplies, and maintaining order in the hardest-hit areas. Volunteers from across the country poured in, bringing food, clothing, and medical supplies. While initiatives were unfolding to support the people lower grade hurricanes hit the region hampering the effort.

The President, in a series of press conferences, reiterated the government's commitment to aid recovery efforts. "We stand with the people of Florida, Louisiana, and Texas," he declared. "We will rebuild stronger and better. No one will be left behind."

As the days turned into weeks, the focus shifted from immediate relief to long-term recovery. Engineers and city planners began assessing the damage and planning the reconstruction of critical infrastructure. The goal was not just to rebuild but to create more resilient communities capable of withstanding future storms. Innovations in building materials and designs were considered to ensure that homes and businesses could better resist hurricane-force winds and flooding.

Economic assistance packages were rolled out to support individuals and businesses. Grants and low-interest loans would help those who lost their homes and livelihoods begin the process of rebuilding. Special attention was given to vulnerable populations, ensuring they received the help needed to recover.

The recovery process raised discussions on climate change and the increasing frequency and intensity of such storms. Scientists and policymakers emphasised the need for sustainable practices and improved disaster preparedness to mitigate future risks. Investments in green energy and infrastructure were proposed as part of the broader strategy to combat climate change and enhance resilience.

Toward the end of the season another major hurricane formed, ominously following the same path as Hurricane Martha. The region, still reeling from the first catastrophe, braced for yet another onslaught. Named Hurricane Nathan, this new storm intensified rapidly, evoking a sense of dread among the battered communities of Florida, Louisiana, and Texas.

Emergency services, already stretched thin from the aftermath of Martha, scrambled to prepare for Nathan. Evacuation orders were issued once again, but many residents, still displaced or recovering from the previous storm, found it difficult to comply. Makeshift shelters were hastily reopened, and supplies were distributed as best as possible. However, the region's infrastructure, weakened by Martha, struggled to support another massive evacuation and relief effort. As Hurricane Nathan made land, the damage was catastrophic. The weakened or destroyed defences in many areas were easily overwhelmed.

Buildings that had barely withstood Martha collapsed under Nathan's relentless force. Floodwaters surged through streets, turning them into torrents that swept away cars, debris, and tragically, people.

The loss of life was devastating, with over one thousand people perishing in the storm.

The storm's impact was felt far inland, wreaking havoc on communities that had believed they were safe. Nathan's torrential rains caused rivers to overflow, flooding areas that had not seen such devastation in living memory. Landslides and mudslides added to the chaos, burying homes, and cutting off entire towns from aid.

In the wake of Nathan, the region faced an unprecedented crisis. The combined devastation of two back-to-back hurricanes left a trail of destruction that seemed insurmountable. Thousands of homes were lost, businesses were obliterated, and critical infrastructure lay in ruins. The emotional toll on the survivors was profound, with many struggling to cope with the compounded loss and trauma.

The federal response was ramped up, with the President declaring a second state of national emergency. More funds were allocated, and a more robust, coordinated relief effort was launched. International aid began to pour in, with countries around the world offering assistance in the form of supplies, manpower, and financial aid.

FEMA, along with the National Guard and countless volunteers, worked to rescue those trapped, provide medical care, and deliver essential supplies. Makeshift hospitals were set up to treat the injured, and mental health professionals were brought in to support those dealing with the trauma of consecutive disasters.

In Washington, discussions urgently took place to discuss the need for more effective climate change policies and disaster preparedness measures. Lawmakers from both parties recognised that the increasing frequency and intensity of hurricanes demanded a reassessment of national strategies for infrastructure resilience and emergency response.

After the season had passed The President visited the region to see the damage for himself and to meet the people. He appeared visibly moved by what he saw and those he spoke to. He reiterated his pledge for as much financial aid as was necessary. The visit was considered a PR coup by the White House team; the President had stepped up to the plate and performed like a Shakespearean actor; the challenge was delivering on all the President had promised.

As the recovery process began, the focus was on not only on rebuilding, but also on learning from the back-to-back hurricanes to better prepare for the future. Efforts to reinforce infrastructure, improve evacuation plans, and enhance early warning systems were prioritised. Communities resolved to build stronger, more sustainable structures that could better withstand the forces of nature.

Hurricane Nathan had compounded the tragedy initiated by Martha, but it also reinforced the determination of the affected regions to come together, rebuild, and emerge stronger. The dual impact of these storms served as a stark reminder of the urgent need to address climate change and invest in resilience, ensuring that future generations would be better protected from the growing threats posed by extreme weather.

The President was often quoted as saying that 'climate change is the most important topic facing the world,' but in private he had other views, and would do all he could to dither and delay America's transition to clean energy. The US economy was fragile, and it would take a brave President to undermine current economic policies such as drilling for oil, in favour of long-term investment in clean energy. Experts had forecast the transition would be costly, bringing about significant unemployment in some areas of the country and the decimation of some industrial sectors in the poorest parts of America where the party relied on votes. The President also knew that China and India to name only two other major polluters were ploughing ahead with the use of fossil fuels and would do so for decades to come. Was America prepared to lead the climate agenda and in doing so undermine its own economy while others prospered? And this was the conundrum. Reducing CO_2 emissions required a global commitment to achieve the kind of effect necessary to meet the scientific community's advice on safe levels of emissions to avoid global warming.

Privately, the President and Congress knew the fight to restrict global warming to a maximum of 1.5c by 2035 was a pipedream, the hope instead was that technology would be developed in time to deliver fast-tracked solutions to the entire world's climate challenges avoiding the known consequences should they fail.

Recent events had put added pressure on the President, and he decided to spend four days at Camp David to recuperate. He left with a small team, including Eleanor, his Chief of Staff, and key advisers.

Before departing, Eleanor and the communications team crafted a statement to the press.

"The President will be working from Camp David over the next few days to develop comprehensive strategies for our ongoing initiatives, he remains fully engaged and committed to his duties and will be in regular communication with senior officials and Congress."

Upon arrival at Camp David, the President and his team took the day off to relax before setting to work. The tranquil setting provided a much-needed break from the chaos surrounding Washington DC, allowing for clear-headed discussions, and planning sessions, but there was little time for the President to rest.

As they worked late into the night, the President insisted. "We need to show the American people that we're not just responding to crises but proactively building a better future. Our actions in the coming weeks will set the tone for the rest of our administration."

The days at Camp David were intense but productive. By the end of the retreat, the team had developed a detailed action plan, complete with timelines, responsibilities, and communication strategies. They felt rejuvenated and ready to move ahead.

Before leaving Camp David, the President recorded a video message for the public. "Over the past few days, I've had the opportunity to reflect and plan with my team here at Camp David. We are more committed than ever to addressing the issues that matter most to you.

We've developed detailed plans to move forward with our economic recovery initiatives and ensure every American has the opportunity of a better life. Thank you for your continued trust and support. Together, we will overcome these challenges and build a brighter future."

The President's return to the White House was met with a renewed sense of purpose. The message from Camp David had been clear: the administration was focused, determined, and fully capable of leading the nation through these turbulent times. Eleanor felt confident that with their refined strategies they were ready to guide the country toward a better future.

Of course, challenges were always lurking. Intelligence filtered through that North Korea was planning another missile test, this time with the capability to decimate South Korea and Japan with nuclear weapons. The Russians were known to be egging them on, offering advice on technology and tactical strategies.

The news was alarming, and the President knew that swift, decisive action was required. He immediately called for an emergency meeting of the National Security Council (NSC)

The President's inner circle, including Eleanor, the Secretary of Defence, the National Security Advisor, and senior military officials, all assembled in the secure conference room.

The President opened the meeting in a sombre tone. "We face a grave threat. North Korea's scheduled missile test egged on by the Russians, could destabilise the entire region and pose a direct threat to our allies. We must address this with a combination of diplomacy, military readiness, and international cooperation."

The Secretary of Defence presented the intelligence reports, detailing North Korea's missile capabilities and the evidence of Russian involvement. The room was tense as they discussed the potential scenarios and the implications for global security.

The following hours were a whirlwind of activity. The President personally called the leaders of South Korea and Japan, reassuring them of the United States' unwavering support and coordinating their responses. Diplomatic channels were opened with China, urging them to exert pressure on North Korea to halt the missile test.

Simultaneously, U.S. military forces in the region were put on high alert. Joint exercises with South Korean and Japanese forces were planned, and additional missile defence systems were deployed to protect against potential threats. The Pentagon worked to ensure that all contingencies were covered.

In New York, the U.S. Ambassador to the United Nations convened an emergency meeting of the Security Council, pushing for a resolution condemning North Korea's actions and calling for increased sanctions.

The international community responded with a show of solidarity, condemning the potential missile test and the involvement of Russia.

The President and his team monitored the situation closely. Eleanor coordinated with the communications team to keep the public informed without causing undue panic. The message was clear: the administration was fully engaged, taking decisive action to protect the nation and its allies.

In the days that followed, the diplomatic efforts began to yield results. China, under significant international pressure, used its influence to persuade North Korea to stand down from the missile test. The threat of additional sanctions and the show of military readiness by the U.S. and its allies also had a sufficient deterrent effect.

Eleanor felt a sense of relief that a temporary calm had descended. The successful handling of the North Korean threat had demonstrated the administration's ability to respond to international crises, but the complexities of global politics meant that challenges would always be on the horizon. It wasn't if but when the next international crisis raised its head.

In recognition of China's intervention, the President thanked the Chinese leadership for their statesmanship, however, only weeks later, intelligence revealed that China was planning an invasion of Taiwan, once again claiming their sovereign rights over the territory. This new development presented a significant geopolitical crisis that threatened regional stability and U.S. interests in the Asia-Pacific region.

The revelation came during a routine intelligence briefing. The atmosphere in the Oval Office was tense as the President, and his senior advisers absorbed the gravity of the situation. Eleanor, always a voice of common sense with a strategic edge, immediately began coordinating an emergency response plan.

The President called another emergency meeting of the National Security Council. The room was filled with top military and intelligence officials, the Secretary of State, and other key advisers. The President began the meeting with a stern tone.

"This is a direct threat not only to Taiwan but to the balance of power in the region and our own strategic interests. We need to respond firmly and decisively." In truth the intelligence they were working on had filtered through following months of attempted efforts by the Chinese to establish talks with the Taiwanese authorities about sovereignty.

The 'Taiwan issue' was a contentious, complicated, and long-standing one. In 1942, after the United States entered the war against Japan, the Chinese government renounced all treaties signed with Japan before that date and claimed Taiwan's return to China's sovereignty. In the Cairo Declaration of 1943, the Allied Powers also declared the return of Taiwan, including the Pescadores, to the Republic of China as one of several Allied demands. The Cairo Declaration however was never signed or ratified. Both the US and the UK later considered it not legally binding. The Chinese, on the other hand, assert it was legally binding and lists later treaties and documents reaffirming the Cairo Declaration in law.

In 1952, Winston Churchill said Taiwan was not under Chinese sovereignty and the Chinese Nationalists did not represent the Chinese state, but that Taiwan was entrusted to the Chinese Nationalists as a military occupation. Churchill called the Cairo Declaration outdated in 1955.

The legality of the Cairo Declaration was not recognised by the deputy prime minister of the United Kingdom, Anthony Eden in 1955, who said there was a difference of opinion on which Chinese authority to hand it over to. In 1954, the United States denied that the sovereignty of Taiwan and the Penghu islands had been settled by any treaties, although it acknowledged that the Republic of China effectively controlled Taiwan and Penghu. In the 1960 *Sheng v. Rogers* case, it was stated that, in the view of the US State Department, no agreement transferred the sovereignty of Taiwan to the ROC, though it accepted the exercise of Chinese authority over Taiwan and recognised the Government of the Republic of China as the legal government of at the time.

One of the challenges recent US governments have had in dealing with international affairs in a global leadership role is fully understanding the historical significance and relevance of past events. Rarely, were historical facts reviewed and considered before making judgements.

Few people with the academic understanding to assist their decision making were hired, and the sovereignty of Taiwan was a case in point.

The Secretary of Defence presented the latest intelligence, which included satellite images showing a build-up of Chinese military forces near the Taiwan Strait. "We have unmistakable evidence that China is preparing for a large-scale invasion. Their forces are mobilising, and this could happen within weeks."

The Secretary of State emphasised the need for a diplomatic response. "Mr. President, we must immediately engage with our allies in the region and reaffirm our commitment to Taiwan. We need to make it clear to China that their actions will have severe consequences."

Eleanor, who had at least some understanding of the history of the region, proposed a multi-pronged approach that included convening an urgent meeting with leaders of key allies, including Japan, South Korea, Australia, and the European Union, to form a united front against China's aggressive actions, engaging with the United Nations to highlight the potential threat to global stability. Despite the need diplomatically to engage with the Chinese acknowledging a complex sovereignty issue prevailed, had to agree there was a need to increase the U.S. military presence in the Asia-Pacific region, including deploying additional naval assets to the Taiwan Strait and enhancing defence cooperation with Taiwan.

From an economic perspective, coordinating with allies to impose targeted economic sanctions on China, aimed at deterring their actions without escalating the conflict into a full-blown trade war was not easy. She acknowledged, like it or not, China was the manufacturing powerhouse of the world, and a major disruption to supply chains would have dire consequences for the US and world economy. She encouraged the President to once again to address the nation and the international community to explain the seriousness of the situation and the steps the US were taking in a leadership role to prevent further conflict and uphold international law.

The President listened intently and agreed with the importance of acting quickly and decisively. "We need to show China and the world that we will not stand by while international norms are violated."

Of course, the President had no knowledge or interest in regional history but the significance of what transpired in the past decades was not lost on the Chinese.

Within hours, the administration launched a full-scale diplomatic offensive. The President personally reached out to allied leaders, securing their support, and coordinating a unified response. A high-level delegation was sent to Taiwan to express solidarity and support.

The Pentagon began increasing its military presence in the region, deploying additional aircraft carriers, submarines, and other naval assets to the Taiwan Strait. Joint exercises with regional allies were scheduled to demonstrate military readiness and deter Chinese aggression.

Simultaneously, the administration worked with Congress and international partners to draft a package of targeted economic sanctions aimed at key sectors of the Chinese economy. These measures were designed to pressure China without causing undue harm to the global economy.

The President addressed the nation from the Oval Office. "My fellow Americans, we are facing a grave threat to the stability of the Asia-Pacific region and the principles of international law. China's planned invasion of Taiwan is unacceptable, and we will take all necessary steps to prevent this aggression and protect our allies. We are working closely with our partners around the world to ensure a strong and unified response. Our commitment to peace, security, and the rule of law remains unequivocal."

The international community responded with widespread condemnation of China's actions. The United Nations Security Council held an emergency session, and although China vetoed any resolutions against it, most member states voiced their opposition to the invasion.

As the situation unfolded, the U.S and its allies maintained a high state of alert. Diplomatic efforts continued behind the scenes, with back-channel communications aimed at de-escalating the situation and finding a peaceful resolution.

In the weeks that followed, the intense diplomatic and military pressure began to have results. Faced with a united front of international opposition and the prospect of severe economic repercussions, China reconsidered its plans for an immediate invasion. The crisis remained unresolved, but the immediate threat of conflict was averted. The Chinese government in response issued a detailed account of history asserting that agreements and accords dating back to the 1940's and 1950's were still legally binding, and it was clear China had sovereign rights over the territory, but their attempt at educating western powers was dismissed without consideration.

President Trent, reflecting on the current situation, knew the crisis was only on hold not resolved, instead of using diplomacy to build bridges with the Chinese to somehow end hostilities permanently, he chose to condemn them in public and in private as opportunists.

Not unlike the Russians, who had broken their promises on several occasions regarding Ukraine, the Chinese irritated that they were not being listened to stepped away from its pledge not to invade Taiwan. On September 4th, Chinese warships landed troops on Taiwanese territory, and a war had begun.

The President was woken in the early hours by a secure call from the National Security Adviser. The news was grim: Chinese forces had initiated an invasion of Taiwan, marking the start of a potentially catastrophic conflict. The President immediately summoned the National Security Council for an emergency session at the White House.

The atmosphere in the Situation Room was electric. Satellite images and real-time intelligence reports were displayed on screens, showing Chinese troops landing on Taiwanese beaches and fierce resistance from the Taiwanese military.

The President addressed the room. "We have entered a critical phase. Our response must be swift, decisive, and coordinated. We cannot allow this aggression to go unanswered."

The Secretary of Defence provided a military assessment. "Mr. President, we have several options on the table. We can increase our naval and air presence in the region to support Taiwan directly.

We should also consider cyber operations to disrupt Chinese command and control systems."

The Secretary of State emphasised the need for immediate diplomatic action. "We need to rally our allies and partners for a collective response. An emergency meeting of the UN Security Council should be called, even if we expect a veto from China. We must also activate our defence treaties with regional allies, particularly Japan and South Korea."

Eleanor suggested a comprehensive approach. "Mr. President, we need to implement a full-spectrum response. Military support for Taiwan, diplomatic efforts to isolate China, economic sanctions to pressure them, and a robust public communication strategy to keep our people informed and maintain international support. That said I believe we should have engaged or listened to the Chinese claims on sovereignty. History is not necessarily on our side."

The President looked quizzically as Eleanor after hearing her final words. Again, he knew nothing of past historical events. He agreed with the general thrust of advice from his advisers and within hours, the U.S. military was mobilising. Aircraft carriers, destroyers, and submarines were dispatched to the Taiwan Strait. Fighter jets and bombers were deployed to bases in the region. Cyber Command launched operations to disrupt Chinese military networks.

The international response was swift. Allies in NATO and the Asia-Pacific region expressed staunch support for Taiwan and the U.S. response. An emergency session of the UN Security Council saw widespread condemnation of China's actions, though as expected, China and Russia vetoed any binding resolution. However, the moral and political pressure on China intensified.

Economic sanctions were announced, targeting Chinese banks, state-owned enterprises, and critical industries. The global economic impact was significant, and the collective resolve of the international community was clear.

As U.S. and allied forces engaged in joint operations with Taiwanese defenders, the conflict escalated. Naval and air battles erupted in the Taiwan Strait, while cyber warfare raged behind the scenes.

The resilience and bravery of the Taiwanese people were evident, as they resisted the invasion with determination.

Eleanor coordinated closely with the President, ensuring that all aspects of the response were synchronised. The administration maintained constant communication with allies, the military, and the public. Regular updates were provided, emphasising the strategic importance of defending Taiwan and upholding perceived international law.

In the weeks that followed, the conflict continued with heavy casualties. The international community remained steadfast in its support for Taiwan. Diplomatic efforts to broker a ceasefire were underway, but the path to peace was fraught with challenges. The Chinese administration knew the US and its allies would not risk a direct military involvement or 'boots on the ground' in the conflict, it would be too high a price to pay. They had already factored in the global condemnation and effects of sanctions and appeared confident they could prosecute their war and win, and over time their occupation of Taiwan would become accepted, albeit not approved of by the global community, just as the Russians had annexed parts of Ukraine prior to the full-scale invasion.

The President and Eleanor knew that the road ahead would be long and difficult, but they remained committed to defending democracy and maintaining global stability. Their leadership during this crisis would define their legacy and shape the future of international relations in an increasingly complex world.

Interestingly for Eleanor, the President's usual default mode for action on the ground involving US troops in such situations was muted. She knew he recognised the might and force of the Chinese military, and an intervention militarily by the US would have disastrous results. It was essential that the US did all in its power to stop the war, but not with boots on the ground.

As the emergency session of the National Security Council continued, Eleanor stressed. "Mr. President, while our support for Taiwan is clear, direct military intervention with ground forces with our allies would escalate this conflict to catastrophic levels. We need to focus on leveraging our strengths: diplomacy, economic pressure, and technological superiority.

It is not too late I believe to fully appreciate the history of this region and why the Chinese are so insistent on their sovereignty of Taiwan."

It was the second time he had witnessed Eleanor reacting this way about the conflict, but this time he felt the need to better understand her concerns. Eleanor spent time giving a chronological statement of events that justified, in her view, the Chinese claim over Taiwan. He listened without interruption and merely said "That was the past, things have changed, we need to move on…" Eleanor was deflated but not surprised that the President would utter such a glib response. He was not an unintelligent man, but he lacked empathy and rarely considered the facts before making decisions, issuing dictates that could have profound consequences.

"Our goal must be to stop this war and restore stability without further loss of life." He said to her.

The Secretary of Defence proposed alternative military strategies. "We can increase our support through air and naval power, provide advanced weapons systems to Taiwan, and intensify our cyber operations. These actions will bolster Taiwan's defence without involving US ground troops."

The Secretary of State added, "We should increase our diplomatic efforts, as Eleanor had advocated, engaging with China through back channels and mediators. Additionally, we need to speak with our allies to present a united front and increase economic pressure on China." Of course, they all knew once China had landed on Taiwanese soil they were there to stay, and no amount of military threats or economic sanctions would budge them.

The President approved the plan, and the administration moved swiftly to implement it. Diplomatic teams were dispatched to key capitals around the world to galvanise international support and coordinate responses. The Pentagon ramped up military aid to Taiwan, ensuring they had the resources needed to defend themselves as best they could.

In Washington, the President addressed the nation once more. "My fellow Americans, we are facing a critical moment. The Chinese aggression against Taiwan threatens global peace and stability.

While we stand firmly with Taiwan, we will not escalate this conflict through direct military intervention. Instead, we will use our strengths in diplomacy, economic pressure, and technological superiority to seek a peaceful resolution to bring an end to this conflict and restore stability to the region."

The international community responded positively, with many nations joining the coalition and reinforcing sanctions against China. Back-channel communications were opened with Chinese officials, seeking avenues for negotiation and de-escalation.

In the weeks that followed, surprisingly, the combined pressure of military support, economic sanctions, and diplomatic efforts began to have an effect. China faced mounting difficulties both domestically and internationally they had not factored in. Protests and economic disruptions within China, coupled with the resilience of Taiwanese defence, created conditions for potential negotiation.

A breakthrough came when a neutral third-party country offered to host peace talks. The President, seeing the opportunity, instructed the diplomatic team to engage fully. Eleanor coordinated closely with the team, ensuring that all aspects of the strategy were aligned and focused on achieving a ceasefire.

The peace talks were tense and complex, but the persistent efforts of the international coalition, combined with the strategic pressure applied by the US and its allies, eventually led to an agreement. China agreed to a cease fire and discussions on a framework for long-term negotiations on the status of Taiwan.

The administration and its allies had navigated an incredibly perilous situation achieving a temporary peace while avoiding the catastrophic consequences of direct military intervention. That said, the Chinese refused to remove their troops from Taiwanese soil until talks had taken place leaving the situation in limbo.

Despite the early signs of progress, the peace talks failed, and China officially claimed Taiwan as their own according to historical agreements they said they would defend in international courts.

They set up command and control systems as they had done in Hong Kong when they legitimately took back the lease on the territory from the British. This was different though. Taiwan, according to international consensus was sovereign territory, won by war, and it was unacceptable, and China would pay a price.

The President and his team were in the Situation Room, grappling with the gravity of the situation. The international community was in uproar, condemning China's aggressive actions and according to them, the illegal annexation of Taiwan. The stakes had never been higher, and the need for a robust, coordinated response was urgent.

Eleanor, worried by the President's reaction in private threatening ground forces and heavy artillery against the Chinese needed to offer the President a multifaceted plan that combined diplomacy, economic pressure, and non-ground military actions to respond effectively without escalating the conflict into a global war.

The President opened the meeting. "China's actions are a direct violation of international law and a threat to global stability. We must respond decisively but careful to avoid further escalation, but I am prepared to issue orders for our forces to engage with the Chinese if necessary."

The President instructed the Secretary of State to immediately convene a summit with key allies, including NATO, the European Union, and major Asian partners like Japan, South Korea, and Australia. The goal was to form a united front and issue a collective statement condemning China's actions and demanding the immediate withdrawal of Chinese forces from Taiwan.

Despite the expected Chinese veto, the U.S. would push for a Security Council resolution condemning the invasion and seek to pass a resolution in the General Assembly, where a broader consensus could be reached. There would also be increased efforts to isolate China diplomatically, urging countries worldwide to sever or downgrade diplomatic and economic ties with Beijing. This would not be easy.

It was agreed to implement a new round of severe economic sanctions targeting key sectors of the Chinese economy, including technology, finance, and energy.

The President tasked the Treasury Department with coordinating these measures with international partners to maximise their impact. They would also explore the feasibility of a partial or full trade embargo against China, focusing on critical goods and services. This would require broad international support to be effective.

Establishing an economic aid package to support Taiwan's government-in-exile and its people, ensuring they had the resources to continue their resistance and maintain their claim to sovereignty was high on the agenda. There would also be a ramped-up U.S. naval and air presence in the region to deter further Chinese aggression and reassure allies. They would conduct regular joint military exercises with regional allies to demonstrate strength and readiness intensifying cyber operations aimed at disrupting Chinese military communications and command systems in Taiwan, but those close to the President knew these measures would not deter the Chinese from remaining as occupiers.

It was becoming a regular exercise. The President would deliver a televised address to the American people explaining the situation, the administration's response, and the importance of supporting Taiwan. This would also serve to reassure the public and maintain domestic support for the administration's actions.

In the following days, the UN General Assembly passed a resolution denouncing the invasion, with overwhelming support from member states.

The President's address to the nation was well-received, rallying public support and reinforcing the administration's commitment to defending international norms and supporting Taiwan.

Despite the failed peace talks, the international community's response, led by the United States, demonstrated a strong, unified front against China's aggression. The situation remained volatile, but the combined diplomatic, economic, and military efforts provided a strategic framework to counter China's actions and support Taiwan's fight for sovereignty. Only Eleanor it seemed had a true understanding of the past and a sympathy for the Chinese claim of sovereignty. Her voice alone would not change the direction of travel the international community had embarked upon.

CHAPTER TEN

PRESIDENTAL ELECTIONS

Presidential elections in the US were underway amidst all the turmoil with Russia, China, and the Iranian proxies. Domestic US politics had taken a back seat in the previous year, inflation remained stubbornly high, and interest rates were crippling the economy. Working people were striking again, and naturally the government and in particular the President were blamed. Eleanor knew how fragile and volatile the President could be and spoke to him about his strategy if he were to fight for a second term. In her heart she hoped, as her inner team hoped, he would decide not to run, but she knew he would. His ego would demand it.

Eleanor's awareness of the political climate and the President's temperament was keenly developed. She knew the President's inclination to run was driven not just by political ambition, but by a deeply ingrained need for validation. With international crises stirring and domestic unrest mounting, she recognised the delicate balance that needed to be maintained.

"Mr. President," Eleanor began cautiously, "Your commitment to leadership during these turbulent times is undeniable. However, we must fully review our options if we are to secure another term. The public's perception is critical, especially with the current economic strain and the ongoing strikes."

The President listened, his expression a mix of determination and fatigue. "Eleanor, we need to show strength and resolve. These challenges are significant, but we've faced worse. We can turn this around."

Eleanor nodded, her mind formulating potential approaches. "We need to communicate a clear plan to tackle inflation and bring down interest rates and further support the working class. Transparency and empathy will be key in connecting with the voters."

The President attempted to cover a yawn. "And our stance on international issues? We can't appear weak."

"Precisely," Eleanor agreed. "We must project confidence without escalating tensions unnecessarily. It's a fine line, but with a solid strategy, we can achieve our goals."

Inwardly, Eleanor hoped the President would reconsider his decision to run, but she knew his ego and drive made it unlikely. Her focus would have to be on guiding him through the complexities of the campaign, aiming to address the nation's concerns while maintaining stability on the global stage. He was mentally and physically tired and Eleanor knew he needed a break. She continued with her advice.

"The key will be balancing domestic concerns with our international strategy. Voters are feeling the pinch of inflation and high interest rates daily.

They need to see that you understand their struggles and have a viable plan to help them." The President leaned back in his chair, his fingers tapping on the desk. "What do you suggest?"

"We need to build on the work that is already being undertaken to support communities. Strategies that not only tackle inflation but also supports small businesses and addresses the strikes. We should propose targeted relief measures and investment in job creation. If we can present a clear, actionable plan, it will resonate with the public."

"And what about foreign policy?" the President asked. "We can't ignore the threats from Russia, China, and the Iranian proxies. We need to show strength."

Eleanor nodded. "Absolutely. Highlighting our efforts to maintain peace and stability will be crucial. At the same time, we need to ensure our military readiness is visible and unequivocal. The public want to see that in addition to the tangible help we will offer them, that we remain the world's leading democratic power working to create a better world."

The President looked closely at her as though he were trying to read her mind. "So, a balanced approach. Addressing economic issues at home while maintaining a firm stance abroad."

"Exactly," Eleanor affirmed. "It's about showing that we are capable of handling multiple crises simultaneously.

We need to communicate your vision clearly and consistently, using every platform available to us."

"Eleanor, I appreciate your insights. I believe we can turn things around."

Eleanor smiled, though her concern for the President's well-being remained. "We can, Mr. President. With the right strategy and a united front, we can win the public's trust again."

As she left the Oval Office, Eleanor felt the weight of the task ahead. Convincing the President to focus on pragmatic solutions rather than impulsive decisions would be challenging. Yet, she was determined to steer the campaign in a direction that would not only give them a fighting chance of winning the election but also address the nation's pressing issues. Despite her unease over the President's suitability in the role it was her job to help him get re-elected and that was what she would do.

Her inner team shared her hope that the President might step aside, but knowing the man she worked for, Eleanor braced herself for a relentless campaign ahead. It was now her mission to ensure that his bid for a second term was not just about ego but about genuine leadership and solutions for the American people

Eleanor's next step was to convene her inner team, the group of trusted advisers who had been with the President through thick and thin. They gathered in the West Wing, a sense of urgency permeating the room. As they settled in, Eleanor addressed her team.

"Everyone, thank you for coming. We're facing an uphill battle, both domestically and internationally. The President has decided to run for a second term, and it's our job to craft a strategy that addresses the challenges head-on and resonates with the electorate."

The team nodded, each member understanding the gravity of the situation. Thomas, the economic advisor, was the first to speak. "We need a bold economic plan. People are struggling with high inflation and interest rates. We should focus on measures like reducing the tax burden on the middle class, increasing subsidies for essential goods, and creating job programs in sectors hit hardest by the economic downturn."

Janet, the communications director, added, "We also need to manage the narrative. The media is ruthless, and we can't afford any mistakes. We should highlight the President's past achievements while laying out a clear, forward-looking vision. The public needs to see that he has a plan and that he's the right person to implement it."

"Agreed," said Michael, the foreign policy expert. "On the international front, we must balance strength with diplomacy. We can't afford to be seen as weak, but we also can't provoke further conflict. We should emphasise our diplomatic efforts with allies and our commitment to international stability. We need to reassure the public that we're on top of these threats."

Eleanor nodded. "Excellent points. We also need to address the strikes and labour unrest. We should engage with union leaders and work towards fair agreements that prevent further disruptions. Showing that we support workers' rights will be crucial."

The team discussed various initiatives and communication strategies, gradually forming a comprehensive plan. As the meeting ended, Eleanor felt a renewed sense of purpose. Despite the challenges, she believed they could turn the tide.

Over the next few weeks, the campaign began to take shape. Eleanor and her team worked day and night, refining policies, prepping the President for speeches, and coordinating with grassroots organisations to rally support. They faced constant scrutiny from the media and relentless attacks from political opponents, but they persevered.

Eleanor spent long hours in the West Wing, often working late into the night. She knew the stakes were high, not just for the President but for the nation. Every decision, every speech, every policy proposal had to be meticulously crafted to address the concerns of the American people.

One evening, as she reviewed the latest poll numbers, the President walked into her office. He looked tired. "Eleanor, I want to thank you for everything you're doing. I know it's not easy."

Eleanor looked up and smiled. "It's my job, Mr. President. We're in this together, and we will succeed."

The President smiled, a rare moment of genuine warmth. "I have no doubt. Let's show them what true leadership looks like."

As the campaign progressed, the President's message began to resonate with voters. His speeches were more focused, his policies more refined. The public started to see him not just as a leader but as someone who genuinely cared about their struggles and had a plan to address them. His campaign coffers began to swell; it was clear there was a desire from key backers they wanted him to win a second term.

The weeks turned into months, and the campaign gathered momentum. Eleanor's team was working like a well-oiled machine, each member contributing their expertise to the cause. They focused on key swing states, where the President's message of stability and resilience could make the most impact.

Eleanor knew they needed a defining moment, something that would shift the narrative decisively in their favour. The opportunity came in the form of a nationally televised town hall. The President would be taking questions directly from voters, addressing their concerns in real-time. It was a high-stakes event, but Eleanor saw it as a chance to highlight the President's connection with the American people.

The preparation was intense. Eleanor and Janet rehearsed potential questions with the President refining his responses. They knew he had to come across as empathetic and solution-oriented, someone who understood the everyday struggles of ordinary Americans. Eleanor knew he was an accomplished actor and could pull it off.

The night of the town hall arrived, and the atmosphere was charged with anticipation. Eleanor watched from behind the scenes as the President took the stage. The questions came one after the other, covering everything from the economy and healthcare to foreign policy and labour rights. The President managed each question with a calm, measured demeanour, his responses reflecting the careful preparation he and Eleanor had undertaken.

One moment stood out. A middle-aged woman, visibly distressed, spoke about her struggles to make ends meet amidst rising costs. "Mr. President, we all work, my family is barely getting by. What are you going to do to help people like us?"

The President leaned forward; his voice filled with compassion. "I hear you, and I understand the challenges you're facing. We have a comprehensive plan to tackle inflation and reduce the burden on working families. We're going to increase support for essential goods, create more job opportunities, and ensure that our economic policies benefit everyone, not just the wealthy. Your concerns are my concerns, and I'm committed to making sure we come through this stronger together. A second term will give us the impetus we need."

Eleanor watched the woman's expression soften, a spark of hope in her eyes. It was a powerful moment, one that resonated with millions of viewers across the country.

After the town hall, the team gathered to review the feedback. The response was overwhelmingly positive. The President's performance had struck a chord, and for the first time in months, the poll numbers began to shift in their favour.

Eleanor allowed herself a moment of relief before diving back into the campaign. There was still much work to be done, but the town hall had given them a crucial boost. They capitalised on the momentum, ramping up their efforts in key areas and doubling down on their message of stability and hope.

In the following weeks, the President's schedule was packed with rallies, policy announcements, and interviews. Eleanor and her team worked to ensure every detail was perfect, every message on point. They faced continuous attacks from opponents and scrutiny from the media, but their focus never waned.

One evening, after a particularly gruelling day, Eleanor received a call from an old friend, a seasoned political strategist who had seen many campaigns come and go. "Eleanor, I have to say, you're doing a remarkable job. The President's message is resonating, and people are starting to believe again."

Eleanor smiled; it was just what she wanted to hear. "Thank you. It's been a tough road, but we're making progress. There's still a lot to do, but I believe we can turn this around."

Her friend's voice was warm. "You already have. Just keep pushing, stay focused, and remember why you're doing this. The people need someone who cares, and they're starting to see that in the President."

As the election day approached, the atmosphere grew even more intense. The nation was on edge, the stakes higher than ever. Eleanor knew they had done everything possible to prepare, but the outcome was in the hands of the voters.

Election night was a blur of activity, the team gathered in the war room, monitoring results as they came in. The tension was palpable, every update bringing a mix of hope and anxiety. Hours passed, and the results began to form a positive graphic. The race was tight, but the President was edging ahead in critical swing states.

Finally, in the early hours of the morning, the news came through. The President had secured enough electoral votes to win re-election. The room erupted in cheers, the months of hard work and relentless effort culminating in a moment of triumph.

They had done it. Against all odds, they had secured a second term for the President. It was a victory not just for the campaign but for the vision of a more stable and resilient America, but could the President deliver it over the next four years? His psychopathy almost brought the world to the brink in his first term, what lay ahead no one could predict.

As the celebrations continued, the President approached Eleanor, a look of gratitude in his eyes. "Eleanor, we did it. Thank you for everything."

Eleanor smiled. "We did it together, Mr. President. Now we need to make sure we deliver on our promises over the next four years." The celebrations had barely concluded when the reality of their situation reasserted itself.

Reports of escalating tensions in Eastern Europe and the South China Sea poured in, and Iranian proxies were ramping up their activities in the Middle East. The President was thrust back into the fray of international diplomacy, even as domestic issues demanded his attention.

Eleanor sat in her office, contemplating her future.

She had been thinking about stepping down as a Special Adviser to return to her professional practice, a role that offered more stability and less stress. But the thought of leaving the President, and the country in such a precarious position weighed heavily on her. She knew the President's mental volatility could surface at any moment, potentially leading to catastrophic decisions.

Her phone rang interrupting her thoughts. It was a message from Thomas, the economic advisor: "Emergency meeting in the Situation Room. 10 minutes."

Eleanor gathered her notes. The moment for reflection had passed, and duty called. She walked briskly to the Situation Room, her mind already shifting to crisis management mode.

The room was buzzing with activity when she arrived. Military advisers, intelligence officials, and key members of the President's cabinet were present. The President himself looked strained.

"Thank you all for attending" the President said as everyone took their seats. "We have multiple crises unfolding simultaneously, and I need everyone's best efforts to manage this situation."

The briefing began with updates from the Secretary of Defence and the National Security Adviser. Russian forces were mobilising in greater numbers than seen before near the Ukrainian border and the intelligence suggested this would be a defining moment for the Ukrainian people. Chinese naval activity was increasing around Taiwan to shore up defences should the US or its allies choose military action to force the Chinese to retreat, and Iran-backed militias were attacking multiple allied positions in Iraq.

Eleanor listened intently, her mind racing through the implications. She knew the President would need careful guidance to navigate these treacherous waters. As the meeting progressed, she took detailed notes and started to formulate a plan.

When it was her turn to speak, Eleanor addressed the room with a calm but authoritative tone. " First, we must communicate our commitment to international stability while emphasising our willingness to engage in diplomatic negotiations.

Second, we need to bolster our alliances, ensuring our partners know we stand with them. Third, we must maintain domestic stability by addressing economic concerns and demonstrating that the government is in control."

The President nodded, appreciating her clear and strategic thinking. "Eleanor, I need you to take the lead on this. Coordinate with the State Department, the Department of Defence, and our economic advisers. We need a comprehensive strategy, and I trust you to deliver it."

Eleanor felt the weight of responsibility settle on her shoulders. She had considered stepping down, but now it was clear she couldn't walk away. The stakes were too high, and her unique understanding of the President's psyche made her indispensable in this critical moment.

"Understood, Mr. President. I'll begin immediately."

The following days were manic with activity. Eleanor worked night and day, coordinating efforts between various departments, drafting strategic communications, and advising the President on every step. She met with ambassadors, briefed congressional leaders, and her team.

Her efforts began to pay off. Diplomatic channels opened, reducing the immediate threat of military escalation. Economic sanctions were carefully targeted to pressure adversaries without harming global markets. At home, new economic measures were introduced to alleviate inflation and support struggling families.

Throughout it all, Eleanor kept a close watch on the President, managing his volatile temperament and ensuring he remained focused. She knew that one wrong move, one impulsive decision, could unravel everything for which they had worked.

One evening, after a particularly exhausting day, the President called her into the Oval Office. "Eleanor, I don't know what we would do without you. Your clear-thinking and guidance has been invaluable."

Eleanor smiled, feeling a mix of pride and exhaustion. "Thank you, Mr. President. We're not out of the woods yet, but we're making progress."

The President nodded. "I know. And I want you to know how much I appreciate your dedication. You could have chosen an easier path, but you stayed. That means a lot to me and to the country."

Eleanor felt a sense of pride. "I believe in what we're doing, Mr. President. We're making a difference, and that's what matters."

As she left the Oval Office, Eleanor knew she had made the right decision to stay. The challenges were immense, but she was committed to seeing them through. For the sake of the American people, and indeed the world, she would continue to navigate the complexities of politics and diplomacy, ensuring that the President remained steady and focused despite his erratic decision making.

CHAPTER ELEVEN

CHALLENGES DOMESTICALLY AND INTERNATIONALLY

The weeks that followed were more pressured than usual. Eleanor's days began before dawn and ended long past midnight. The crises abroad showed no signs of abating, and the domestic situation remained precarious.

One Thursday morning, Eleanor found herself back in the Situation Room. The latest intelligence reports indicated that Russian forces had finally mobilised for another major incursion into Ukraine and were ruthlessly attacking the critical infrastructure that remained in major towns and cities including Kyiv; hundreds more civilians had perished and just as many displaced. Electricity, water, and gas lines were destroyed making an unbearable life even more bleak. The Ukrainian President begged the international community, and especially the US, to deploy troops and use weaponry to directly attack invading Russian forces as they were overwhelmed. It was accepted within military circles both in the US and internationally that no matter how much military hardware Ukraine was given it required troops on the ground in large numbers to have the kind of impact that would see Russian troops withdraw. Numerous Russian troops reportedly deserted. Of course, the Ukrainian President call for troops to be deployed on the ground was the last thing Eleanor and her team wanted to hear, knowing the President's instinct was to comply.

"We can't allow the President to deviate from our previously agreed strategy," the Secretary of Defence commented in the Situation Room meeting. "We need to avoid direct conflict at all costs."

Eleanor spoke up. "We need to show strength without escalating to direct conflict. Let's focus on bolstering our presence in Eastern Europe and we should ramp up diplomatic efforts to de-escalate the situation."

The President had remained quiet listening to his teams' assessment of the intelligence but now he spoke.

"For the past two years at least we have employed diplomacy with the Russians, the Chinese, the Iranians and where has it got us? They are taking us for fools. The plea from the Ukrainian President makes sense to me. I should call the Russian President and make it very clear that unless they withdraw their troops and cease bombing key infrastructure we will, and I emphasise will, send in our troops and a level of firepower they have never seen before."

The room was silent as echoes of the Iraqi invasion rushed through people's minds. The President looked at the assembled gathering one by one. Nobody flinched. There was a deafening silence.

Eleanor spoke up. "Mr President. We all understand your frustration, but I think, with respect, you underestimate what we have achieved using diplomacy in each of these conflicts.

I agree we have not resolved the issues, far from it, but an act of aggression in the way you describe would make us feel good, but the fallout, the long-term impact would be catastrophic as it was in Vietnam and more recently in Iraq and Afghanistan, and lead to a possible nuclear war. We should not under-estimate the lengths the Russian President would go to if we acted. He is mentally unstable and unchallenged politically, and I say that authoritatively.

Again, there was silence in the room as the President stared at the ceiling formulating his response. "Thank you, Eleanor, for your advice. If I am not to issue an order for direct action, I need you and your team to come up with a plan that does more than offer diplomacy, I need to approve a strategy that will force the Russian's, the Chinese and the Iranians to take us seriously, otherwise I fear the world will descend into chaos and there will be no going back."

After the meeting, and faced with an impossible challenge, Eleanor called her inner team together. They divided tasks, with Thomas focusing on economic sanctions and Janet preparing communications strategies. Michael, the foreign policy expert, worked on strengthening alliances and coordinating with international partners.

Eleanor's days were consumed by negotiations, briefings, and strategy sessions.

She spoke with ambassadors, military leaders, and economic experts, weaving a complex web of responses designed to stabilise the situation on all fronts.

One evening, as she reviewed the latest reports, she received an urgent call from the National Security Advisor. "Eleanor, we have credible intelligence that an Iranian proxy is planning a major attack on one of our bases in the Middle East."

Eleanor's heart sank. Another crisis. "We need to move quickly," she said. "We need increased security measures at all bases in the region. And let's prepare a strong but measured response."

The hours that followed were intense. Eleanor coordinated with military commanders, briefed the President, and crafted statements for the press. The attack was prevented, and the administration's swift response was praised. But the sense of constant threat was wearing on everyone. Every new revelation brought the prospect of the President issuing direct orders for military action closer.

During these international crises, domestic issues could not be ignored. Inflation was still high, and the worker strikes were intensifying. Eleanor knew they needed to address these concerns to maintain public support.

She called a meeting with key economic and employment advisers "We need to find common ground," she said. "People have legitimate grievances, and we need to show that we are listening and willing to act."

The administration announced a series of measures to support workers, including wage increases and better working conditions. It was a significant step towards easing domestic tensions but had the inevitable impact on government finances.

As the days turned into weeks, Eleanor continued to juggle the myriad demands of her role. She was constantly on the move, attending meetings, making calls, and managing crises. She barely had time to sleep, let alone think about her original plan to step down.

One evening, as she was about to leave the West Wing, she received a call from her friend, the seasoned political strategist.

"Eleanor, you're doing an incredible job. But you need to take care of yourself. I can see from a distance the pressure you are under isn't sustainable."

Eleanor sighed. "I know. But there's so much at stake. I can't walk away now."

Her friend paused. "Just remember, even the strongest leaders need to rest. The country needs you at your best."

Eleanor knew her friend was right. She promised herself she would find a way to balance her responsibilities better. But for now, there was no time to slow down.

The next major challenge came in the form of a cyberattack on critical US infrastructure. The attackers targeted power grids and communication networks, causing widespread disruptions. The intelligence pointed to state-sponsored actors from a rival nation.

Eleanor convened an emergency meeting with cybersecurity experts and national security advisers. "We need to establish who was responsible and respond decisively," she said. "First, let's secure our networks and restore services. Then, we need to send a clear message that such actions will not be tolerated."

The response was swift and coordinated. Cybersecurity teams worked to mitigate the damage and reinforce defences. The President addressed the nation, reassuring the public and condemning the attacks.

In private, Eleanor worked on diplomatic channels to address the cyber threat. She engaged with allies to coordinate a collective response and applied pressure on the suspected state actors through backchannels and official statements. Of course it was no surprise the Russians were responsible. The US were not the only target. The UK and Germany had also suffered with major disruptions.

One evening as Eleanor walked through the quiet corridors of the White House, she came across the President in a hallway. "Eleanor, you've been fantastic through all of this. I don't know what we would have done without you.

Eleanor smiled she was genuinely touched by his comment. "Thank you, Mr. President. It's been a team effort. And there's still much to do." The President smiled and unusually chose to embrace her.

She responded and wondered what had motivated him to do so. Eleanor the psychiatrist, not the President's Special Adviser concluded he saw in her the one individual that had steered him away from ill-thought-through actions that would have had dire consequences and removed him from office. She was his political lifeline. She had considered stepping down, but now she knew she was exactly where she needed to be; at his side ensuring his Presidency steered a course that would provide security for the nation.

In a bizarre turnaround from a week earlier when the President thanked her for her contribution and hugged her, she noticed a troubling shift in the President's attitude toward her. He started questioning her decisions more frequently, often in a condescending tone. His comments became increasingly critical, and he took pleasure in undermining her authority in front of others.

One afternoon, after a particularly tense meeting where the President had openly questioned her judgment on a key foreign policy issue, Eleanor retreated to her office, her mind racing. She had always known the President could be volatile, but this was different. His behaviour was becoming more erratic and unpredictable, and it was affecting not only her but the entire inner circle.

She knew she had to address the situation before it spiralled out of control. She needed to find a way to manage the President's growing psychopathy and ensure that his decision-making did not lead to catastrophic consequences.

She sought the counsel of Dr Alan Thompson, a friend and a renowned psychologist who had worked with high-profile political figures in the past. Eleanor trusted his judgement and expertise. A discrete meeting was arranged.

"Alan, thank you for meeting with me at such short notice,"

"Of course, Eleanor. I'm always here to help."

"The President's behaviour has become increasingly erratic in the last week.

He's questioning my decisions constantly, undermining my authority with my team, and his comments have become more personal and critical. I'm worried this could lead to poor or even disastrous decision-making."

He nodded thoughtfully. "It sounds like the President's stress levels have increased, and he may be feeling threatened by your competence and independence. This can trigger defensive and hostile behaviour, especially in someone with psychopathic tendencies."

"Do you have any advice?" Eleanor asked, feeling a mix of frustration and desperation. "I need to manage this situation without escalating it further."

"First, maintain your professionalism at all times. Do not react emotionally to his provocations. Stay calm and composed and focus on the facts and logic behind your decisions. Second, try to create a support network within the administration. Identify key allies who can help buffer the President's behaviour and provide you with a united front."

Eleanor nodded, taking mental notes. "I have a close network of advisers on board, but I'm worried his behaviour will escalate. Up until now I have managed to control any irrational behaviour, but the dynamic has changed, he no longer sees me as his closest ally?"

"In that case, you may need to consider more direct intervention," He paused momentarily.

"This could involve a frank conversation with the President about his change of behaviour or discussing the situation with other senior members of the administration to find a collective solution."

Eleanor left the meeting worried, knowing Dr Thompson was right, but he revealed nothing new, nothing she hadn't already assumed about the President.

Despite her efforts, the President's attitude toward her continued to deteriorate. During a critical meeting with military advisers, he dismissed

Eleanor's concerns about a proposed military action, insisting on a more aggressive approach.

Eleanor knew this decision would have dire consequences, but she also knew challenging him directly in front of others could backfire.

After the meeting, she approached the President privately. "Mr. President, I need to speak with you about our strategy. I'm deeply concerned about the potential repercussions of the proposed action."

The President glared at her. "Eleanor, I'm tired of your constant second-guessing. If you can't get on board with my decisions, maybe you shouldn't be here."

Eleanor felt a mix of emotions but kept her composure. "I'm here at your request to ensure we make the best decisions for the country, Mr. President. My concerns are based on expert advice and our long-term strategic goals."

The President's eyes narrowed. "Fine. But remember, I make the final decisions. You may offer advice, but you do not command."

Eleanor left the conversation feeling frustrated and angry, and if she were prepared to admit it, hurt by his coldness, a feeling she rarely experienced. She knew she had to find a way to mitigate the President's increasingly reckless behaviour. She convened a meeting with Janet and Thomas, briefing them on the situation and seeking their support.

They all agreed the President was becoming a genuine problem in maintaining good governance but produced no innovative ideas on how to control him.

CHAPTER TWELVE

ORDER TO ASSASSINATE THE RUSSIAN PRESIDENT

In the weeks that followed, Eleanor tried to restrict her time with the President hoping his stance toward her would change, or at least mellow. She thought long and hard about her encounters with him trying to establish what had changed his mind set, but was unable to pinpoint an incident, a conversation or an action on her behalf that would have triggered the situation she now found herself in. At a time when he needed her counsel the most, he was pushing her away. Fortunately, thus far at least, he had not made any irrational decisions or issued any Presidential orders that endangered the nation.

Weeks passed and the Special Advisers Eleanor worked with carefully managed the President's ego while she remained in the background. They presented their advice in a way that appealed to his sense of control, however, Eleanor feared this was not a sustainable long-term solution.

One evening, after another exhausting day, Eleanor sat in her office, reflecting on the situation. She knew that managing the President's behaviour was a temporary fix. The administration needed a more permanent solution to ensure the President's volatile tendencies did not jeopardise the country's future.

As she considered her options, Eleanor decided to continue her efforts in the background while preparing for the possibility that more drastic measures might be necessary. She would do whatever it took to protect the nation, even if it meant confronting the President knowing she might be sacked.

It was early one Wednesday morning when Eleanor's phone rang. "Emergency meeting in the Oval Office. Immediately." Her heart raced. She knew something significant had happened, but nothing could have prepared her for the gravity of what she was about to hear.

As she entered the Oval Office, the atmosphere was tense. Key advisers and senior officials were already gathered, their expressions a mix of confusion and concern. The President sat at his desk his face grim with determination.

"Thank you all for coming at such short notice. I've made a decision that will change the course of our foreign policy strengthening our stance on global security."

Eleanor glimpsed at others in the room who shared her unease at what was about to be said.

The President slowly opened and closed his eyes several times as though to set the scene. "Last night, I gave the order for our special services to assassinate the Russian President."

The room erupted with gasps and low-level chatter. Eleanor felt her blood run cold. This was not just a reckless decision; it had the potential to unleash an international crisis and military aggression by their adversaries, and the use of nuclear weapons.

Despite her current disharmonious relationship with the President, she provided an immediate response.

"Mr. President," she began, trying to keep her voice steady, "This is an unprecedented move with far-reaching consequences to the point where we could be under nuclear threat from our enemies. I beg you to rescind your order and fully consider the repercussions."

The President's eyes narrowed. "I've considered the repercussions. The Russian President is a threat to global stability. This action is necessary to protect our interests and those of our allies. We need to show everyone that the US is the world's superpower and is prepared to take difficult but necessary decisions. "

Eleanor tried to steady her thoughts as those around her waited for her next intervention.

"Mr. President, an assassination could lead to a significant uncontrolled escalation. We need to explore every diplomatic avenue before resorting to such an extreme measure. We are not like the Russians; we're a law-abiding democracy with an elected leader not an autocrat running the country."

Before the President had time to respond, the Vice President spoke up, his voice firm. "Eleanor is right Mr President. We need to weigh the geopolitical fallout. This could destabilise the entire world order and lead to unforeseen consequences."

The President's face hardened. "I've made my decision. The order stands."

Eleanor exchanged a worried glance with colleagues who looked equally alarmed. "Mr. President," Eleanor tried again, "we must consider the international laws and the precedent this sets. It undermines our moral and legal standing. The US cannot be branded a pariah. Undertaking such an action would solve nothing other than to undermine our credibility as a democratic nation. Acts of this kind are the fodder of despots."

The President slammed his fist on the desk. "Enough! This is not up for debate. I've given the order, and it will be carried out." His face was white with anger; he turned to face the window hands behind his back ignoring everyone in the room.

Eleanor knew she had to act quickly. She needed to find a way to stop this before it was too late. She motioned for several of her colleagues to follow her out of the Oval Office.

Once they were in a more secluded setting, they considered who the President would have instructed to conduct the assassination, they assumed he would have spoken to the head of the CIA. Eleanor decided she needed to speak with him, there was no time to waste.

They all agreed. Eleanor added. "We also need to bring in the Secretary of Defence and the intelligence chiefs. They need to understand the gravity of this decision and provide their input. I will contact them preparing a brief for the National Security Council. We need to present a unified front and provide the President with a clear picture of the potential consequences."

As they worked frantically to assemble the necessary officials and prepare their arguments, Eleanor's mind weighed up the possible outcomes. She knew they were running against the clock, but she also knew they had to exhaust every avenue to prevent a disaster.

The emergency session of the National Security Council was tense. Military leaders, intelligence officials, and key cabinet members were briefed on the situation. Eleanor presented the potential consequences, emphasising the risks of escalation and the importance of diplomatic solutions. The Head of the CIA had indeed been given orders to assassinate the Russian President, but so far had taken no action understanding the gravity of the situation. He had only days to report back to the President that the mission had been accomplished.

The following morning The Secretary of Defence arranged an immediate meeting with the President in the Oval Office along with other advisers. Eleanor thought it best she stayed away believing it would undermine what needed to be said. The Secretary of Defence spoke. "Mr. President, we, your advisers, believe your order to assassinate the Russian President must be rescinded. We must consider the wider ramification of such an action. The potential for retaliation is high, and it could draw us into a wider conflict and importantly undermine our integrity as a world power that upholds the rule of international laws."

The President looked around the room, his expression unreadable. Finally, he spoke. "I hear your concerns. But the Russian President will not stop in his efforts to reclaim Ukraine, he will challenge us on NATO borders and likely Poland will be his next target. We need to remove him now not later. He's a psychopath!" Eleanor had changed her mind and entered the Oval Office just hearing the President's final words. '…A psychopath' it was ironical that he was accusing the Russian President of suffering the same condition he suffered. The thought was not lost on Eleanor, who chose to speak next.

"Mr. President, with respect, we understand the threat, but there are other ways to address it. Sanctions, diplomatic pressure, and covert operations that do not involve assassination. We can collaborate with our allies to isolate and weaken his position without resorting to such drastic measures. I know, we all know, that fulfilling your order will, and I repeat, will have the most severe consequences for world order and our people will suffer."

There was a long silence as the President considered her words. Finally, he looked Eleanor squarely in the eyes. "I'll rescind the order for now. But I need a plan in place to swiftly cripple the Russian President and his cronies.

I want concrete proposals on my desk within 3 days, is that understood?"

As they left the room everyone felt a wave of relief wash over them. Eleanor looked at the President and smiled courteously. "Thank you, Mr. President. We'll get to work immediately."

As the meeting adjourned, Eleanor knew they had only bought themselves limited time. The President's volatility remained a constant threat, and they needed to be prepared for any future aberrations. But for now, they had averted a potentially catastrophic action, and that was a victory.

The President's impulsive nature and growing psychopathy made him a volatile leader, capable of making rash decisions that could endanger global stability. Eleanor needed to ensure that the team remained observant and report any controversial decisions the President made.

The following morning, Eleanor met with the White House team to draft comprehensive strategies to address the threats posed by the Russian President without resorting to assassination. They worked late into the night, developing several ideas involving new economic sanctions, diplomatic pressure on the Russian top table advisers, and covert operations to better understand the regime's plans.

Eleanor also proposed a series of high-level diplomatic engagements to build a coalition against Russian aggression and a social media campaign to alert the Russian people to the damage their President was inflicting on Ukraine and disrupting world order.

When they presented the plan to the President, he listened carefully, his expression inscrutable. After a long pause, he finally nodded. "It's not what I want, but we'll run with it but understand this: if these measures don't produce results quickly, we'll need to revisit more direct actions."

Eleanor and her team left the room, once again they had won the President over but for how much longer?

Eleanor contacted the relevant departments and international allies to put the plan into effect. They also initiated a social media campaign to tell the Russian people the damage their President was inflicting on Ukraine and the international condemnation their country was attracting. The next few weeks were intense for everyone in the White House team.

Despite their efforts, the President's erratic behaviour continued to be a concern. He often second-guessed their strategies, demanding quick results and displaying impatience. Eleanor had to constantly manage his expectations while ensuring that the administration stayed on course. She had re-established a renewed relationship with the President, but it was more formal now, and she had to choose her words more carefully to avoid his ire or her sacking.

One evening, as she reviewed the latest intelligence reports, Eleanor received a call from Sarah, her deputy. "Eleanor, we have a problem. The President is meeting with a group of military advisers privately. He's talking about reactivating the assassination plan." Eleanor could barely contain her frustration.

She thanked Sarah and immediately called her inner team for an emergency meeting. They needed to act quickly to prevent the President from making another reckless decision.

As they gathered in Eleanor's office, Thomas spoke first. "Somehow, we must get ahead of this. If the President is determined to take this route, we need to produce some new and innovative ideas that will persuade him to a different course."

Eleanor agreed. After discussing various scenarios for an hour Eleanor agreed to prepare a briefing for the President and request an immediate meeting."

Eleanor, Janet, and Thomas entered the Oval Office as the President sat at his desk arms folded signifying that he was already in a defensive mode. Eleanor began her presentation. "Mr. President, we are aware that you are again considering the assassination of the Russian President." The President uncrossed his arms and left forward with a stern look on his face. Before he had time to speak, Eleanor continued. "…We have gathered extensive data on the potential fallout of an assassination if that order were to be given. Our allies are deeply concerned about the repercussions and are totally against such an action and strongly advising against such a move, believing it would severely destabilise the world"

She laid out the evidence meticulously, showing projections and intelligence reports that highlighted the risks.

Janet and Thomas reinforced her points, emphasising the diplomatic and economic measures that were already showing signs of success.

During this time, the President listened, his face frozen with anger. Finally, he spoke, his voice intimidating as he barked his words. "Who told you about my meeting with our military advisers? Who instructed you to discuss my plans with our allies?" They said nothing knowing he had more to say. "…I am the elected President, and my orders are to be obeyed. You have all failed me. You come to me with half-baked plans of diplomacy but none of it works. Our allies think we're weak, our adversaries are laughing at us, we need decisive action irrespective of the consequences."

Those last few words 'irrespective of the consequences' echoed in Eleanor's head. This was a psychopath talking. The same psychopath she first met in the Oval Office a few years earlier. He was a danger then and now he had secured a second term in office was an even greater threat.

Eleanor met the President's gaze steadily. "Mr. President, decisive action doesn't have to involve assassination. We can ramp up our current efforts, intensify diplomatic pressure, and increase our support to opposition groups within Russia who could be subtly encouraged to undertake the assassination themselves. Of course, even if his own people were to undertake this task, there would be repercussions as speculation surfaced believing that the US or a western nation was behind the act.

The room fell silent as the President wandered the room. After what felt like an eternity, he responded. It was clear to Eleanor that the President knew he could not execute his order to assassinate the Russian President and had to back down without damaging his ego.

"Again, I will back off our people assassinating the Russian President, but I want you to work with the opposition leaders in Russia with the prime objective of encouraging them to assassinate him.

I want his head on a platter and soon." He showed them the door.

Eleanor felt relieved and exited the room with her colleagues without uttering a further word.

In a moment of relief and perverse humour, Eleanor imagined a headline in the broadsheets of the world's leading newspapers and media outlets 'US President issues Executive order – 'I want the Russian Presidents head on a platter' and wondered how that would go down in Congress and with the wider public. The President would approve of it no doubt. She laughed to herself.

She knew they had only bought more time. The President now wanted the assassination to happen but through a different route. She felt distinctly uneasy.

In the following weeks, increased sanctions and diplomatic pressure started to strain the Russian President's regime, while covert support to opposition groups within Russia began to create internal challenges for his leadership while pressure on an assassination became a distinct possibility. Protests in Red Square gained significant support as the Russian people seeing the social media campaign began to question and challenge the actions in Ukraine.

The President's demands for quick results continued, but Eleanor managed to keep him focused on the broader strategy, using every opportunity to reinforce the long-term benefits of their approach, and that every effort was being made with opposition parties to remove their President. President Trent was pleased to see the Red Square protests on media channels and insisted the campaign be ramped up. The Kremlin had suspected the American's of awakening the Russian people and threatened retaliation.

Late one evening Eleanor received a message from the Secretary of Defence. "Eleanor, we have some significant intelligence. Can we meet?"

At three in the morning, they gathered in a secure room, where the Secretary briefed her on new intelligence indicating that the Russian President was facing increasing dissent within his own ranks. There were signs that his grip on power was weakening, and an assassination was possible.

"This is promising," Eleanor said. "We need to capitalise on this and increase our efforts to support the opposition within Russia. If we can amplify their efforts, we may be able to expedite the process without direct intervention.

It's clear the media campaign we're running is having the desired effect."

The Secretary agreed, a plan would be formulated to ramp up support to the opposition, while also preparing for potential fallout if the situation escalated.

As they implemented their plan, the pressure on the Russian President continued to mount. Eleanor remained vigilant, knowing that the situation was still precarious. She continued to manage President Trent's expectations, keeping him informed and engaged while ensuring that the administration's actions remained measured and strategic.

For once, he could see the plan was working to destabilise the Russian President and his closest allies, but he also knew that dissent in Russia came with consequences for the people. His hope remained that one of their own would assassinate the President saving him from the fallout of issuing an order himself.

As the weeks passed, dissent within Russia intensified, leading to a severe crackdown by the Kremlin. The government's measures become increasingly draconian to suppress the growing unrest and security around the President became watertight. It was a well-known fact that the Russian President's security team were wealthy individuals, made wealthy by their leader in return for unequivocal loyalty, loyalty that meant they would willingly give up their own lives to protect their boss.

A leading US broadsheet provided a rolling commentary on the chaos unfolding in Russia.

'The Russian government in the Kremlin has enacted stringent measures to quell the burgeoning dissent. These measures included:

- Demonstrations are met with lethal force. Protesters in Red Square are shot, and hundreds are arrested.

- Members of opposition parties are rounded up and imprisoned without trial, indicating a complete disregard for legal processes and human rights.
- Foreign journalists, particularly from the US and UK, are arrested and accused of espionage. This is an attempt to control the narrative and prevent the international community from gaining insights into the internal turmoil.
- In response to a US-led social media campaign, Russia launches a significant cyber-attack targeting key installations. The impact is widespread, affecting
- critical infrastructure, including hospitals and government offices all disrupted, impeding essential services.

The cyber-attack extended to the Pentagon, utility installations, banks, and insurance companies, highlighting Russia's capability and willingness to engage in cyber warfare.

With the country on the brink of anarchy, the Red Army is deployed to restore order. However, this move has mixed outcomes:

Army recruits, already stretched thin by the ongoing conflict in Ukraine, begin to desert in significant numbers. This desertion weakens Russia's ability to maintain its military engagements and assert control internally.

Sensing a coup due to the instability, the President is provided with increased security protection. This heightened security underscores the precariousness of the government's hold on power.

The international community watches closely as the situation develops. Key concerns include:

The arrest and imprisonment of protesters and opposition figures without trial raise serious human rights concerns.

The cyber-attack on US installations represents a significant escalation in cyber warfare, potentially prompting retaliatory measures and increasing global tensions.

The disruptions caused by the cyber-attacks and internal unrest have far-reaching consequences:

The attacks on banks and insurance companies cause economic instability, both within Russia and globally.

Relations between Russia and Western countries, particularly the US and UK, deteriorate further, complicating diplomatic efforts and international cooperation.

The report concluded:

'The situation in Russia is rapidly deteriorating, with the government's harsh measures failing to quell dissent and instead exacerbating unrest. The international ramifications of the crackdown and cyber-attacks are significant, potentially leading to a broader conflict necessitating a coordinated global response to address the unfolding crisis. The situation in Russia has significant implications for both domestic stability and international relations. The Kremlin's repressive measures are pushing the country towards greater chaos. The international community faces a complex challenge in responding to Russia's actions, balancing the need for human rights with the risks of escalating cyber warfare. As events unfold, strategic, measured responses will be crucial in navigating this multifaceted crisis.'

Eleanor and her team's relief at the unfolding chaos in Russia underscored the complex interplay of international relations, strategic planning, and crisis management. The internal instability in Russia temporarily diverted the President from considering extreme measures, allowing for a period of strategic respite, but she knew instability in Russia made the world a more dangerous place not a safer one.

Eleanor stood in the Situation Room, her eyes glued to the large screen displaying the latest satellite images and intelligence reports from Russia. The news was grim but expected.

Protesters filled Red Square, their chants for freedom echoing through the historic plaza. The Kremlin's response was swift and brutal with shots fired, hundreds arrested, and opposition leaders rounded up.

Foreign journalists, especially those from the US and UK, were not spared. The Russian authorities accused them of espionage and arrested them, effectively silencing any external reporting on the unfolding chaos.

Eleanor knew this move was as much about controlling the internal narrative as it was about sending a message to the West: Russia would not be cowed. The likelihood of opposition parties in the country had been sufficiently depleted making an assassination impossible.

As if the crackdown weren't enough, Russia launched a massive cyber-attack on key US installations. Hospitals' networks crashed, government offices were paralysed, and even the Pentagon found its systems under siege. The attacks spread to utilities, banks, and insurance companies, causing widespread disruption and panic.

In the Oval Office, the President debated the next steps. Direct military action? A risky assassination attempt? Eleanor shuddered at the thought. Both options carried enormous risks and potential for catastrophic fallout. In raising these options, she knew the President had not learnt a lesson and never would while he remained in office.

"Maybe a retreat to Camp David would help," Eleanor suggested quietly to the Chief of Staff. "The President needs time to think without the immediate day to day pressures."

The idea was quickly approved. The President, weary from the constant barrage of crises, welcomed the respite. "Unless there's another emergency, I don't want to be disturbed," he instructed, heading for the helicopter.

For Eleanor and her team, this was a welcome reprieve. They could finally catch their breath and reassess the situation. The President's absence from the immediate decision-making process meant fewer rash decisions and more time to formulate a comprehensive response.

At Camp David, the President found some peace.

Surrounded by the tranquillity of the retreat, he took long walks, reflecting on the best course of action. Meanwhile, back in Washington, Eleanor and her team were hard at work. Intelligence reports were analysed, strategies were debated, and contingency plans were drawn up.

The chaos in Russia had inadvertently provided a strategic advantage. The President's focus on immediate drastic measures had waned, giving the team the breathing room they needed.

Eleanor coordinated with international allies, ensuring a unified response to Russia's cyber aggression and human rights violations.

Eleanor knew that the key to addressing the crisis lay in international coordination.

She reached out to NATO allies, organising a summit to discuss collective responses to Russia's actions. Sanctions were tightened still further, and cybersecurity measures were strengthened. The international community's condemnation of Russia's crackdown on dissent grew louder. Immediate steps were taken to gain the release of foreign journalists but to no avail. They would be used as pawns in future negotiations.

Behind the scenes, Eleanor and her team continued to support opposition groups within Russia. Covert channels were established to provide them with the resources they needed to continue their struggle. The aim was to weaken the Kremlin's grip from within while applying pressure from the outside.

CHAPTER THIRTEEN

ISRAEL BOMBS GAZA

As weeks turned into months, the situation remained volatile. The Kremlin's hold on power seemed tenuous, with internal factions and military desertions adding to the instability. The international community's unified stance began to show results. Sanctions bit hard, and Russia's economy faltered further. As in often the case the Kremlin's crackdown on its own people bore fruit. Fewer rallies were seen on satellite images and descent started to waver. A sort of exaggerated normality returned to everyday life in Russia and the President remained alive and in power.

Eleanor watched the developments with a mixture of relief that the political scene was settling in Russia, and the threat of a wider conflict had subsided, but also disappointment that the Russian President remained in power able to once again to destabilise world peace.

Amidst the international turbulence, a surprising development unfolded on the home front—the US economy began to show signs of robust growth. Interest rates were reduced, easing the cost of living for many Americans. Consumer confidence surged, and the stock market responded positively. The sense of economic stability was a welcome respite from the chaos abroad.

Eleanor sat with her closest advisers, reviewing the latest economic data. "It's time to capitalise on this," she said. "The President should tour the country, reinforcing our plans for growth and stability."

The idea was met with unanimous approval. Not only would it bolster public confidence, but it would also provide the President with a much-needed break from the relentless challenges in the White House and minimise the danger that he could again go off at a tangent and risk everything.

The President, known for his charismatic presence and masterful oratory skills, was enthusiastic about the tour.

Eleanor coordinated the tour meticulously. The itinerary included major cities and smaller towns across the country, ensuring that the President's message reached a broad audience. Each stop was carefully planned to highlight local industries, job growth, and economic improvements.

The President's speeches were a masterclass in communication. In Chicago, he spoke about the resurgence of manufacturing and the importance of innovation. In Detroit, he addressed the motor industry's growth of electric vehicles and the new jobs it created. In Texas, he highlighted the energy sector's advancements and the move towards sustainable energy sources.

At each location, the crowds responded enthusiastically. The President's message was clear: the government's policies were working, and the country was on a path to prosperity. His presence and words instilled a renewed sense of hope and confidence.

Back in Washington, Eleanor monitored the public's reaction closely. Polls indicated a significant increase in the President's approval ratings. The media coverage was overwhelmingly positive, with commentators praising the President's leadership and vision.

Eleanor noted the shift in public sentiment. The tour not only highlighted the economic gains but also helped to unify the nation in a time of global uncertainty. The President's visibility and the personal connection he forged with the American people were invaluable.

While the President toured the country, Eleanor and her team continued to manage the day-to-day challenges. The situation in Russia remained volatile, but the international coalition's efforts were beginning to show results. The Kremlin, under immense pressure, started to show signs of concessions and some foreign journalists were released and deported.

Eleanor knew that the battle was far from over, but the domestic stability provided a stronger foundation from which to address international issues. The economic growth and public confidence gave the administration the political capital needed to manoeuvre through the complex global landscape.

The President returned to the White House rejuvenated and more popular than ever. The tour had not only boosted the nation's morale but also reminded the President of the support and trust placed in him by the American people.

Eleanor briefed him on the latest developments. "The tour was a success," she said. "Your speeches resonated deeply, and we're seeing a surge in public support. We've bought ourselves some time and goodwill."

The President nodded, understanding the significance. "Good. Now let's use this momentum to tackle the challenges ahead, both at home and abroad."

Eleanor reflected on the recent months. The chaos in Russia, the cyber-attacks, and the economic challenges had tested their resolve. But through strategic planning, effective communication, and the President's chaotic leadership, they had navigated the storm.

Just as the US was beginning to enjoy a period of economic growth and renewed public confidence, a new international crisis erupted. Eleanor's sense of foreboding returned as intelligence reports detailed the assassination of the Iranian President. Accusations against Israel flew swiftly, despite their vehement denials.

The situation deteriorated rapidly. Hezbollah, acting as Iran's proxy, seized control, and launched hundreds of missiles into Israeli territory. The devastation was immense hundreds of innocent civilians were killed despite Israel's defence systems intercepting most of the missiles.

The Israeli response was swift and fierce, launching retaliatory strikes deep into Iran. The region was plunged into chaos, and the possibility of a full-scale war loomed large.

In the White House Situation Room, the President convened an emergency meeting with his top advisers, including Eleanor. The atmosphere was tense as they gathered around the table, the gravity of the situation evident on every face.

"Reports are coming in from all over," said the National Security Advisor. "Hezbollah's attacks have caused significant casualties, and Israel's response has been devastating. We're looking at a potentially protracted conflict here."

The President turned to his advisers. "We need a strategy.

We cannot let this escalate into a broader regional war, but we also need to stand by our allies and ensure our own security."

Eleanor spoke up. "Our first step should, as always, be diplomatic. We need to engage with our allies and the UN to call for an immediate ceasefire. At the same time, we should ramp up our intelligence operations to understand who exactly orchestrated the assassination and why."

The Secretary of Defence spoke. "We should also consider positioning our forces in the region as a deterrent. Show that we are prepared to intervene if necessary."

As the team worked through the night, Eleanor coordinated with international allies. Calls were made to the leaders of key nations, urging them to support a ceasefire and de-escalation. The UN Security Council was convened for an emergency session.

Meanwhile, US intelligence agencies were put on high alert, tasked with uncovering the true perpetrators behind the assassination. The situation was further complicated by the volatile reactions from various factions within Iran and its allies.

After intense diplomatic efforts, a tentative ceasefire was brokered, but it was clear that the situation remained unstable. The US deployed additional naval and air forces to the region as a show of strength and support for its allies.

Eleanor briefed the President on the latest developments. "The ceasefire is holding for now, but tensions are incredibly high. We need to maintain pressure on both sides to adhere to the ceasefire while continuing to seek a longer-term solution."

The President agreed. "We also need to reassure our own people. This situation could easily spiral out of control, and we need to be ready for any eventuality."

The President prepared to address the nation. In his speech, he acknowledged the gravity of the situation while emphasising the importance of diplomacy and stability.

He reassured the American public that the administration was committed to maintaining peace and supporting its allies.

Eleanor watched the President deliver his speech with the same confidence and poise that had won over so many during his recent tour. The message was clear: the US would not be drawn into another war without exhausting all diplomatic options first.

Despite the temporary ceasefire, the region remained a powder keg. Eleanor and her team worked to balance the immediate needs of the crisis with longer-term strategies for peace and stability. They engaged with international partners, sought to mediate between conflicting parties, and prepared for all outcomes.

The assassination of the Iranian President had thrown the Middle East into turmoil, but through careful diplomacy and strategic planning, the US aimed to prevent a full-scale war. Eleanor knew that in politics, positive outcomes were often fleeting, but she was determined to work through this new crisis with her inner team.

As if the situation weren't dire enough, the conflict escalated further. Following a series of devastating attacks by Hamas, Israel had entered Gaza, initiating a prolonged military campaign against the faction and its supporters. The conflict resulted in significant civilian casualties and widespread destruction, devastating the already fragile territory.

With Hezbollah now actively engaging from the north and Hamas from the south, Israel found itself fighting on two fronts. Both factions, backed by Iran, intensified their attacks, and the region teetered on the brink of a full-scale Middle East war.

The implications were clear: if not contained, the conflict could spill over, drawing in other nations and leading to a broader, more catastrophic war. The global community watched with growing concern, fearing the repercussions of such a conflict.

In Washington, the President convened another urgent meeting with his top advisers, including Eleanor. The gravity of the situation was clear as they gathered in the Situation Room.

"The escalation in the Middle East poses a significant threat not only to regional stability but also to global peace," the National Security Advisor began. "We need a comprehensive strategy to address this crisis."

Eleanor added, "Our first priority, as always, should be to broker a ceasefire and prevent further escalation. At the same time, we must address the humanitarian crisis in Gaza and work with international partners to provide relief and support."

The US launched a robust diplomatic campaign. The President reached out to key allies in Europe and the Middle East, urging them to join efforts to de-escalate the conflict. The Secretary of State was dispatched to the region to meet with Israeli and Palestinian leaders, as well as other stakeholders.

At the United Nations, the US led efforts to pass a resolution calling for an immediate ceasefire and humanitarian aid for Gaza. The resolution faced opposition but garnered enough support to pass, underscoring the international community's desire for peace.

While diplomatic efforts continued, the humanitarian situation in Gaza worsened. Eleanor coordinated with NGOs and international aid organisations to expedite the delivery of food, medical supplies, and other essential resources to the affected population.

"We need to ensure that humanitarian aid reaches those in need," Eleanor emphasised during a meeting with relief organisations. "This is not just a political issue; it's a moral imperative."

In parallel with diplomatic and humanitarian efforts, the US increased its military presence in the region as a deterrent. Naval ships were deployed to the eastern Mediterranean, and additional troops were stationed at key bases.

After weeks of intense negotiations, a fragile ceasefire was finally brokered. The fighting subsided, but the region remained tense and unpredictable. The ceasefire provided a temporary respite, allowing humanitarian aid to flow into Gaza giving diplomats a chance to work towards a more lasting peace.

Eleanor felt relieved but knew that this was only a temporary solution. The underlying issues remained unresolved, and the potential for renewed conflict was ever-present.

The crisis in the Middle East highlighted the fragile nature of global stability and the constant need for vigilant diplomacy. Eleanor and her team faced immense challenges but remained committed to finding a path to peace.

The situation in Gaza rapidly deteriorated once more. Israeli troops and armoured units advanced, and the relentless bombardment decimated the territory. The civilian toll was staggering, with half a million displaced and tens of thousands killed. The images and reports from the ground painted a grim picture.

While the US pledged unwavering support to Israel in its efforts to eliminate Hamas, not all nations shared this stance. European allies expressed deep concern over the humanitarian crisis, calling for an immediate ceasefire and urging both sides to return to the negotiating table.

Amidst the turmoil, President Trent undertook a secret mission to Jerusalem. The aim was ambitious: to meet with Israeli leadership and broker a peace deal that could halt the bloodshed. The President's visit was shrouded in secrecy, with only a handful of top advisers, including Eleanor, aware of the details.

In Jerusalem, President Trent met with Prime Minister Benjamin Weissman. The discussions were difficult and fraught with tension. The President appealed for a humanitarian ceasefire and proposed a framework for peace that included security guarantees for Israel and humanitarian relief for Gaza.

Despite President Trent's efforts, his overtures were subsequently ignored. The Israeli leadership, emboldened by strong domestic support and determined to eliminate the threat of Hamas, rejected the proposed ceasefire. The offensive continued unabated, and the humanitarian toll grew ever more severe.

Back in Washington, Eleanor faced the daunting task of managing the fallout from the failed diplomatic mission.

She knew that the administration needed to rebalance its strategy, weighing up the need to support a key ally with the growing international condemnation and humanitarian concerns.

Eleanor convened a meeting with senior advisers to reassess their approach. "We need to maintain our support for Israel, but we cannot ignore the humanitarian crisis unfolding in Gaza," she said. "Our credibility and moral standing are at stake."

The advisers debated options, from increasing humanitarian aid to Gaza to applying diplomatic pressure on Israel to halt its offensive. It was a delicate balance to strike, given the strong pro-Israel sentiment within parts of the administration and Congress. Israel had closed the borders making humanitarian aid almost impossible to deliver. People were starving. Utilities were non-existent, and a million people were at risk.

The administration decided to significantly ramp up the call for humanitarian aid to Gaza, but the call was ignored. Eleanor coordinated with allies to ensure that the aid that did reach those in need was distributed fairly but even this proved an impossible task as trucks delivering aid were hijacked and set alight.

At the same time, the US intensified its diplomatic efforts, urging Israel to consider a ceasefire and return to negotiations. The goal was to find a path to peace that addressed Israel's security concerns while also alleviating the suffering in Gaza.

Despite the setbacks, Eleanor and her team continued their efforts behind the scenes. There were small signs of progress, some international leaders expressed support for a humanitarian ceasefire, and a few influential voices within Israel began to call for a re-evaluation of the military strategy.

The Gaza conflict highlighted the profound challenges of navigating international crises where strategic alliances, humanitarian concerns, and diplomatic efforts intersect. Eleanor and her team faced immense pressures, but their relentless pursuit of a balanced and principled approach underscored the complexity and necessity of responsible global leadership. The path to peace was uncertain, but every effort to alleviate suffering and promote dialogue was a step towards a more stable and humane world.

Soon after President Trent's return from Israel, Eleanor and key members of the administration gathered in the Oval Office for a debrief on his trip. The atmosphere was a mix of urgency and anticipation, with international turmoil contrasting sharply against promising domestic developments.

President Trent recounted his discussions with Israeli leadership, detailing the challenges and the firm stance they encountered. "Despite our best efforts, they are not ready to consider a ceasefire," he said, his frustration evident. "We need to reassess our approach and continue pushing for a balanced resolution."

Eleanor nodded, then moved to domestic news. "While the international situation remains complex, we have some positive news on the home front," she began, signalling to the Economic Adviser to present the latest data.

"Mr. President, the economy is growing at an impressive rate. Unemployment is down, consumer confidence is up, and we're seeing significant growth across multiple sectors." The room buzzed with a renewed sense of optimism.

"Our economic outlook is very positive," the adviser continued. "This gives us room to consider tax cuts and increased investment in key projects. These moves could further stimulate growth and reinforce public confidence in our administration."

Eleanor expanded on the proposed plans. "We have identified several key areas for potential investment: infrastructure, education, and renewable energy.

These projects will not only create jobs but also lay the foundation for long-term economic stability and growth."

The discussion then turned to tax cuts. The Secretary of the Treasury outlined a proposal aimed at providing relief to middle- and lower-income families while incentivising businesses to invest and expand.

"These tax cuts will put more money in the pockets of everyday Americans," the Secretary explained. "Combined with our investment projects, this will create a virtuous cycle of growth and prosperity."

President Trent listened intently, weighing the information. "We have a unique opportunity here," he said. "But we must balance our domestic agenda with our international responsibilities. We cannot afford to lose sight of the situation in the Middle East."

Eleanor agreed. "Our domestic success gives us leverage on the international stage. A strong economy at home strengthens our position and credibility abroad. We need to use this to our advantage, continuing to push for peace and stability while ensuring our own prosperity."

A press release was circulated to the media.

'We are experiencing unprecedented growth in our economy. This is a testament to our collective efforts and the resilience of the American people. We will continue to invest in our future, ensuring that every American benefits from our nation's prosperity. We are working to bring stability and peace to the Middle East. Our efforts are grounded in the belief that diplomacy and humanitarian aid are crucial to resolving conflicts.'

In the days following the administration rolled out detailed plans for the proposed tax cuts and investment projects. Public reaction was overwhelmingly positive, with many praising the administration's balanced approach to fostering economic growth while addressing international crises.

The administration's ability to navigate the dual challenges of international conflict and domestic growth showed its resilience and strategic capability.

CHAPTER FOURTEEN

PRESIDENTIAL SCANDAL REVEALED

Days later, Eleanor received a phone call from a trusted source informing her that a scandal was about to unfold involving the President. The scandal was the President's affair with a young woman and the two children she had given birth to. Both allegedly fathered by the President.

Eleanor's heart sank as she processed the call from her trusted source. The information about the impending scandal involving the President was both shocking and devastating. It was well-known that the President had been married for years, and upon taking office, he and his wife had agreed she would not take on the traditional duties of the First Lady. She preferred to stay out of the limelight, focusing on their private life rather than the public spectacle.

The scandal, however, was about to shatter that private life. This revelation threatened to not only undermine his personal life but also his political career and the trust of the nation.

Eleanor knew she had little time. The news was bound to hit the headlines soon, and the President would need to address it head-on. Damage control was essential. The first step would be to confirm the facts with the President and understand the full scope of the situation. She needed to discuss how to manage the media, the public's reaction, and the political fallout.

She considered the potential responses: a public apology, a private settlement, or even a resignation. Each option had its own set of consequences. The affair itself would be a blow to his image, but the existence of two children made it a much more complex issue.

Eleanor also thought about the young woman and her children and the President's wife. They would be thrust into the spotlight, subjected to intense scrutiny and harassment. Protecting them while navigating the political storm was a delicate balance that needed careful consideration.

As the minutes ticked by, Eleanor felt the weight of the responsibility on her shoulders.

This scandal had the potential to redefine the presidency, and how they managed it would be critical in determining the future.

First, she decided to contact the President directly. It was crucial to verify the information and understand his side of the story before any action could be taken. She needed to know if he was aware of the impending scandal and if he had any plan in place.

As she phoned the President's private line, she mentally prepared herself for the difficult conversation. The phone rang twice before he answered, his voice calm but with an undertone of tension that hinted he might already be aware of the storm brewing.

"Mr. President, it's Eleanor. We need to talk immediately. I've received some disturbing information that requires your urgent attention."

There was a pause on the other end of the line. "I assume this is about the affair," the President said quietly.

"Yes, and the children," Eleanor replied. "We need to discuss how to manage this before it becomes public. Have you confirmed the details?"

The President sighed deeply. "Yes, it's true. I was hoping to resolve it quietly, but it seems that's no longer an option. We need to talk."

Eleanor felt a degree of empathy for the man who now seemed vulnerable. "We do. The first step is to consult with our legal and PR teams. We need to prepare a statement and decide on our next moves."

"I understand," the President said. "I'll gather the necessary people. Let's meet in the Oval Office in an hour."

As she hung up, Eleanor quickly began drafting a plan. She called the Chief of Staff, the Press Secretary, and the President's personal lawyer, requesting their immediate presence. They needed to discuss the legal implications, the media strategy, and the potential political fallout.

When they convened, the atmosphere was tense. Eleanor outlined the situation, emphasising the urgency and the need for a cohesive response.

"We have three main options," she began. "First, the President can issue a public apology, acknowledging the affair and the children. This might gain some sympathy but also risks intense media scrutiny and public backlash. Second, we could negotiate a private settlement with the woman involved, though this could be seen as a cover-up if discovered. Lastly, the President could consider resigning, but this would be a drastic step with its own set of repercussions."

The room was silent as they weighed the options. The Press Secretary was the first to speak. "A public apology might be the best course. It's honest, and we can frame it as the President taking responsibility for his actions."

The lawyer nodded. "Legally, an apology is sound, but we must ensure that the President's statement is carefully crafted to avoid any admissions that could lead to further legal issues."

The Chief of Staff looked grim. "The political fallout will be severe, but honesty might salvage some trust with the public. We need to be prepared for an attack from the opposition and media."

Eleanor took a deep breath. "Then with your consent Mr President we will prepare a public statement. We need to control the narrative as much as possible."

As they worked on the statement, Eleanor's thoughts turned again to the young woman and her children, and indeed the President's wife. They needed protection and support. She made a mental note to arrange for their safety and privacy, understanding that their lives would be forever changed by this revelation.

Hours later, the President stood before the cameras, his expression sombre.

Eleanor watched as the President faced the nation, delivering his carefully crafted apology. His voice was steady, but he was more emotional that she thought he would be.

"My fellow citizens," he began, "I come before you today with a heavy heart.

I must acknowledge and apologise for a serious lapse in judgment on my part.

I have engaged in an extramarital affair, and two children were born from that relationship. This is a deeply personal matter, but given my position, I understand that it has significant public implications."

He paused, letting his words sink in before continuing. "I have let down my wife, my supporters, and the nation. I accept full responsibility for my actions and the pain they have caused. I am committed to making amends and working to rebuild the trust you have placed in me."

The President's apology was brief and came across as sincere. As the cameras stopped rolling, Eleanor felt a mix of relief and anxiety. The first step was taken, but the challenge lay ahead.

The media reaction was immediate and intense. Headlines were dramatic, pundits debated the implications, and social media lined up with opinions. As expected, the opposition seized the opportunity to criticise the President, calling for his resignation and questioning his ability to lead.

Eleanor and the team had anticipated this. They had a plan in place for media engagement. The Press Secretary conducted follow-up briefings, emphasising the President's willingness to take responsibility and his commitment to transparency. Trusted allies in the media were briefed to help shape a positive tone and accountability.

Behind the scenes, Eleanor worked to manage the fallout. She coordinated with the President's wife, ensuring she was supported and shielded from the media as much as possible. She had no idea of his infidelity. Their relationship was strained, but they presented a united front, understanding the necessity of maintaining stability during the crisis.

Eleanor also reached out to the young woman involved in the affair. It was a delicate conversation.

She expressed the President's commitment to ensuring the well-being and privacy of her and the children. They discussed arrangements for financial support and legal protections.

Eleanor assured her that their priority was to minimise the impact on her life and to protect the children from the public eye.

Meanwhile, Eleanor kept a close watch on the political landscape.

She met with key advisers and allies, rallying support for the President. They emphasised his dedication to public service and the steps he was taking to rectify his personal failings. Some were supportive, understanding the human aspect of the scandal, while others were more hesitant, worried about the long-term damage to their political agenda.

Days turned into weeks, and the initial frenzy began to settle. The President continued his duties, focusing on key policy issues to demonstrate his commitment to the nation. Eleanor also spearheaded a new initiative to address ethical standards within the administration, aiming to restore public trust. The President publicly endorsed this initiative, signalling his dedication to personal and political reform. It was a strategic move to shift the focus from the scandal to positive actions and future goals.

In the months that followed, the scandal gradually faded from the forefront of public consciousness. The President's approval ratings slowly recovered as his actions spoke louder than his past mistakes. Eleanor's efforts had helped to steer the administration through one of its darkest times, and while the scars of the scandal remained, they had managed to avoid a complete disaster.

As the dust settled on the scandal, Eleanor received another call that threatened to upend their fragile recovery. Four women had come forward, claiming they had been in relationships with the President during his marriage, albeit before he took office. They had combined forces and instructed a lawyer to seek damages from the President. This new revelation posed a significant threat to their efforts at rebuilding trust and stability. Eleanor felt a familiar knot of anxiety in her stomach as she processed the news. She knew this would reopen old wounds and create new challenges. The team needed to act swiftly and decisively.

First, Eleanor called an emergency meeting with the President and core advisers. As they gathered in the Oval Office, the atmosphere was heavy with tension.

"Mr. President, we have a serious situation.

Four women have come forward, alleging past relationships with you during your marriage. They are seeking damages through a lawyer."

The President's face paled. "More scandals... this will destroy everything we've been working to rebuild. None of it is true, I want you to understand that."

Eleanor looked directly in the President's eyes. "We need to confirm the facts and understand the full scope of these allegations. We also need to prepare a legal and public relations strategy immediately."

The President's personal lawyer, who had been briefed before the meeting, spoke up. "I recommend we meet with the lawyer representing these women as soon as possible. We need to understand their demands and see if a settlement can be reached discreetly there is no point fighting their allegations that will drag the President into a long and damaging media show." The President agreed, Eleanor was convinced he was guilty and had agreed to settle because he didn't want to defend the indefensible.

The Press Secretary added, "We should also prepare that this will go public. We need to have a statement ready and a plan to manage the media response."

Eleanor agreed. "We'll need to ensure the public knows we're managing this transparently and responsibly. We can't afford any perception of a cover-up."

With the initial plan in place, Eleanor coordinated with the legal team to arrange a meeting with the lawyer representing the four women. She also began drafting potential public statements, emphasising accountability and the steps the administration was taking to address the situation. The meeting with the women's lawyer was tense but professional.

Eleanor and the President's lawyer listened carefully as the allegations were detailed. The women claimed emotional distress and reputational damage, seeking substantial financial compensation.

The President's lawyer negotiated firmly, aiming to reach a settlement that would avoid a prolonged legal battle and further public scandal.

It would be on the basis that the President would deny any wrongdoing. After hours of negotiation, they reached a tentative agreement on a settlement, contingent on confidentiality clauses to protect the privacy of all parties involved.

As the legal team worked out the final details, Eleanor turned her attention to the public aspect. She knew they couldn't keep the story from breaking, but they could control the narrative.

Predictably, the media response was intense. Headlines once again were damning, and pundits speculated on the long-term implications for the President's career. The opposition renewed calls for his resignation, citing a pattern of behaviour unbecoming of a leader.

Despite the relentless pressure, the President continued his duties demonstrating his commitment to his role. Gradually, the media anger began to subside, although the shadow of the scandals lingered.

With conflicts persisting with the Russians in Ukraine, the Chinese in Taiwan, and the Israel-Gaza region, the latter spreading across the Middle East with tit-for-tat missile exchanges between Israel and Iran and Iranian proxies – Hezbollah and Hamas- the President knew that intense diplomatic activity was essential to avoid widening hostilities. He proposed a bold initiative to his inner team: a Summit in Switzerland, inviting the leaders of the countries involved in conflict to discuss ways to resolve or at least reduce hostilities.

The President's advisers were wary. They gathered in the Situation Room to discuss the proposal.

"Mr. President, we understand your commitment to peace," began the Secretary of State, "but this summit could backfire. The stakes are incredibly high, and a failure could exacerbate tensions rather than alleviate them."

The National Security Advisor nodded. "We need to consider the potential repercussions. If the summit fails, it could undermine our credibility and embolden our adversaries."

The President leaned forward and stared at the NSA.

"I understand the risks, but we cannot continue with the status quo. These conflicts are causing untold suffering and instability. We need a new approach."

Eleanor, ever the pragmatic strategist, spoke up.

"Mr. President, if we proceed, we must ensure the summit is meticulously planned. We need clear objectives, contingency plans, and robust support from our allies. We can't afford any mistakes."

The President indicated his approval. "We need to ensure that this summit is a platform for genuine dialogue and progress."

Over the next few months, Eleanor and the team set to work to prepare for the summit. They coordinated with diplomats, briefed allied leaders, and devised comprehensive strategies to manage the complexities of the negotiations.

The President's vision for the summit was clear: it was not just about resolving specific conflicts but about creating a framework for ongoing dialogue and cooperation. He envisioned a series of meetings, starting with Switzerland and continuing regularly to address various global issues. All the invitees were offered diplomatic immunity as some were facing international arrest warrants and could be detained upon arrival in a state that had signed up to the accord. Many were sceptical the invitation to leaders of conflict countries would agree to attend, but they were proved wrong.

The summit's agenda included discussions on the Ukraine conflict, China's occupation of Taiwan, supervised nuclear enrichment with Iran, and the humanitarian crisis in Gaza. Each topic required careful handling and a nuanced approach to ensure productive dialogue.

The location, Switzerland, was chosen for its longstanding tradition of neutrality and diplomacy.

The Swiss government was supportive, offering their facilities and assistance to ensure the summit's success.

As the summit approached, the President addressed the nation, explaining his vision and the importance of this diplomatic effort. He emphasised that this was a crucial step towards global stability and peace, appealing to the public's desire for a safer world. Eleanor knew the President's original idea and desire for this summit to take place was more about stroking his ego rather than the substance or outcomes that everyone else in the team hoped for. Despite that knowledge about the President she hoped, indeed prayed his initiative would work.

When the leaders of Russia, China, Israel, and Iran arrived in Switzerland, the atmosphere was charged with anticipation. The world watched closely, with hopes and fears intertwined. Few thought the summit would get off the ground.

The opening session was tense, the President's spoke passionately about the need for mutual respect and cooperation, urging the leaders to look beyond their differences and work towards common goals and world peace. Only months earlier the President wanted the Russian leader's head presented on a platter.

Discussions were challenging, with moments of contention and disagreement. However, the presence of neutral facilitators, respected Swiss diplomats, helped keep the conversations on track.

Eleanor played a crucial role behind the scenes, coordinating with the President and his team to address emerging issues and adapt their strategies. She consulted with the media to ensure accurate reporting, emphasising the summit's objectives and progress.

After days of intense negotiations, the summit concluded with the statement:

'While the discussions did not resolve existing challenges it marked a significant step towards dialogue and cooperation. Agreements were reached on several key issues, including humanitarian aid for Gaza, a framework for nuclear negotiations with Iran, and commitments to future talks about Ukraine, and Taiwan sovereignty.'

The President addressed the world from Switzerland, expressing cautious optimism. "This summit is a beginning. We have taken the first steps towards dialogue and cooperation. It will not be easy, and much work lies ahead, but we are committed to pursuing peace and stability for all."

Understandably, the response was mixed, but there was a sense of hope. The summit had not been a resounding success, but it had not failed either. It was a foundation upon which to build.

The President's initiative had taken a significant step towards fostering global dialogue.

The road ahead was still fraught with challenges, but they had demonstrated a commitment to peace and diplomacy and the US were seen as an honest broker.

Months later, a second summit was convened, but the reality on the ground in each of the conflicts remained grim. The President's team questioned the validity of holding another summit, sceptical about its potential effectiveness given the lack of tangible progress on the ground, however, the President was determined to pursue this path, insisting on drawing up an agenda that would seek commitments from each power to step back from hostilities.

In the lead-up to the summit, Eleanor and the team faced a daunting task. They needed to craft an agenda that was both ambitious and realistic, one that would push the leaders towards actionable commitments while acknowledging the complexities of each conflict.

The agenda focused on four key areas:

1. Ukraine Conflict: The President aimed to secure a long-term ceasefire agreement and establish a framework for peace talks between Russia and Ukraine.
2. Taiwan: He sought a commitment from China that it would engage in genuine talks about sovereignty and long-term relationships. It was universally accepted China would not withdraw from the territory.
3. Iran's Nuclear Program: The goal was to revive and expand the nuclear deal, with Iran agreeing to enhanced inspections and limitations on its nuclear activities in exchange for a cease in funding for proxies such as Hamas and Hezbollah. This too was

considered by the President's team to be unrealistic. Iran was not about to become an ally of the West.
4. Israel-Gaza Crisis: The President aimed to facilitate humanitarian aid and initiate direct negotiations between Israel and other regional governments with a personal stake in seeing peace established and maintained.
5. As the summit in Switzerland approached, the atmosphere was charged with a mix of hope and uncertainty. The world watched closely, aware of the high stakes involved.

The opening session was formal and tense. The President, addressing the assembled leaders, reiterated his vision for peace and the urgent need for de-escalation of conflict around the world.

"Today, we stand at a crossroads," he began. "The conflicts we face threaten not just our nations but the stability of the entire world. We have a responsibility to our people and to future generations to seek peace. This summit is our opportunity to take meaningful steps towards that goal. Together we could be allies resolving the issues facing the world, not adversaries pulling in different directions."

The initial discussions were challenging, with each leader bringing their own grievances and demands to the table. However, the President's persistence and commitment to dialogue gradually began to create a more cooperative atmosphere.

Throughout the summit, Eleanor coordinated behind the scenes managing communications with the media, emphasising the significance of the summit and the President's dedication to peace. No one in the media believed it would be possible to bring these leaders together under one roof let alone make any tangible progress.

One of the main turning points came during a private meeting between the US President and the Russian leader. It was cordial but the atmosphere was tempered with distrust. The US President emphasised the humanitarian toll of the Ukraine conflict and proposed a temporary ceasefire to allow for meaningful humanitarian aid to flow and peace talks to start. After hours of intense negotiation, the Russian leader tentatively agreed to discuss a ceasefire, marking a significant, albeit cautious step forward but it was clear he had no intention of withdrawing his claim to territory already occupied.

This would be a deal breaker, but the US President put that demand to one side for later discussions.

Similarly, discussions with China led to an agreement to establish a bilateral committee to address the issue of sovereignty of Taiwan. Already occupying the territory put the Chinese in a strong position, and the President knew they were unlikely to walk away from their prize. Despite those significant hurdles it still made sense, at least in the Presidents mind, to stay the distance.

The negotiations with Iran were equally complex, but eventually, a framework was agreed upon to allow Iran to continue with its nuclear programme only for power generation and not enrichment for building nuclear warheads, but it would come with enhanced inspections, and in return they would agree to stop launching missiles into Israel either directly or through its proxies.

The most challenging discussions were around the Israel-Gaza crisis itself. While a long-term peace seemed elusive, both sides agreed to a temporary reduction in hostilities to facilitate humanitarian aid, with further talks planned to address underlying issues. It was clear the Israelis would not accept Hamas being in any way involved in the future of Palestine. A two-state solution was a possibility, but the terms the Israelis envisioned would certainly be rejected by the Palestinians, whoever was in charge.

As the summit ended, the President addressed the assembled leaders and the world. "We have made progress today, but we must remain committed to the path of peace. These agreements, tentative as they are just the beginning. We must continue to work together, to engage in dialogue, and to take concrete actions towards ending these conflicts. World Peace was better than World War. "

The joint statement issued at the end of the summit outlined the commitments made by each leader. While it was clear that much work remained, the agreements reached provided a glimmer of hope.

CHAPTER FIFTEEN

CONFLICT IN AFRICA

Returning to Washington, Eleanor and the team felt a cautious optimism. The second summit had not been an unequivocal success, but it had achieved meaningful steps towards de-escalation in several critical areas. The President's determination and the team's hard work had kept the dialogue alive and demonstrated a commitment to pursuing peace through diplomacy.

The summit galvanised the President and his team, but they knew it was a long and winding road. Each tentative agreement required diligent follow-through to ensure that the commitments made in Switzerland translated into real changes on the ground.

The President called a meeting with his inner circle to discuss the next steps. Eleanor, the Secretary of State, the National Security Adviser, and other key advisers gathered in the Oval Office.

"Ladies and gentlemen," the President began, "We've taken important steps, but we must now focus on implementation and ensuring agreements made are upheld, collaborating with our Swiss partners as independent arbiters. I need your best efforts to keep this momentum going."

The Secretary of State outlined the immediate actions needed. "First, we need to send diplomatic teams to each region to monitor compliance and support the local negotiations. We'll also need to engage our allies to ensure they're backing these efforts. Multilateral pressure can help ensure commitments are honoured."

The National Security Adviser added, "We should also establish clear communication channels with each country involved. This will help us address any issues that arise quickly and prevent misunderstandings."

Eleanor spoke up, "We also need a robust media strategy.

We must keep the public informed about the progress we're making while managing expectations.

Transparency will be key to maintaining support for these diplomatic efforts. Of course, we must accept that some players will not see the US as honest brokers so we must lean on the Swiss as independent arbiters to support our endeavours."

The President nodded. "Let's get started. We can't afford to lose the ground we've gained."

In the weeks that followed, Eleanor coordinated a series of diplomatic missions including Swiss representatives. Special envoys were dispatched to Russia, China, Israel, and Iran to follow up on the summit agreements and ensure that each country was taking the promised steps.

In Ukraine, the ceasefire held, allowing humanitarian aid to reach affected areas. This fragile peace provided a window for more comprehensive peace talks, facilitated by international mediators. The President regularly spoke with the leaders of both Russia and Ukraine, urging them to continue their efforts towards a lasting resolution.

In China meetings were held to outline the process for resolving maritime disputes, the occupation of Taiwan, all with the aim of reducing tension and establishing accords. Eleanor ensured that U.S. support for this process was visible, demonstrating the administration's commitment to regional stability.

Negotiations with Iran over its nuclear program resumed under the agreed framework. Enhanced inspections and new limitations on nuclear activities were critical steps towards rebuilding trust. The President and his team worked closely with European allies to support these negotiations and ensure a unified approach.

In the Israel-Gaza region, the temporary reduction in hostilities allowed humanitarian aid to flow into Gaza. While a long-term peace agreement was still a distant goal, these initial steps created a foundation for further dialogue. Eleanor worked with Middle Eastern diplomats to facilitate ongoing discussions and build on the fragile progress made.

Throughout this period, Eleanor also managed the administration's communication strategy.

She ensured regular updates were provided to the media and the public, highlighting successes, and addressing setbacks honestly. This transparency helped maintain public support and built trust in the President's diplomatic efforts.

Despite measurable progress, significant challenges remained. There were moments when tensions flared, threatening to undo the fragile agreements. In those moments, Eleanor's steady leadership and the President's commitment to establish lines of communication were crucial. They worked diligently to address each issue.

Months passed. The President, addressing the nation once more, reflected on the journey they had undertaken. "We have made significant strides towards peace around the world, but we must remain vigilant. The path to lasting stability is long and we'll encounter obstacles, but with perseverance and dedication, we can have influence. Our commitment to diplomacy and dialogue will continue to guide us as we work towards a safer, more peaceful world."

The President's vision and the teams' collective efforts had brought the world a step closer to peace. Eleanor had to keep reminding herself how the President had transformed from war monger to peace maker, but knew his newfound role was a temporary mindset, he could flip at any moment.

Despite the concerted efforts of everyone in the President's team and the contribution of the international community, the forecast on the international stage remained grim and the continent of Africa was now under the spotlight as a specific area of concern.

Intelligence suggested that forty million people across the region had been displaced in the past few years representing a thirteen percent increase on previous estimates. More than seventy seven percent internally displaced within their countries.

Many of the sixteen African countries in conflict stretched from the western Sahel through the Horn of Africa, encompassing the Lake Chad Basin and Great Lakes regions, and was a reminder of the impact these conflicts have on regional stability.

In Sudan, the clash between the army and the main paramilitary force had caused civilians to flee the violence into six neighbouring countries, many of which were already grappling with their own or other rounds of regional instability.

The conflict between the Sudanese Armed Forces and the Rapid Support Forces had caused an estimated 4.5 million people to flee their homes. It also sparked renewed fighting, including possible ethnic cleansing in the Darfur region, this adding to years of instability caused by decades of military government; Sudan had now surpassed the Democratic Republic of the Congo (DRC) as the country with the largest level of forced displacement in Africa, with 7.3 million people homeless.

Sudan's neighbours, already straining under their own crises, had been saddled with absorbing those fleeing from Sudan—none more so than South Sudan. A quarter of a million South Sudanese refugees in Sudan had been forced to return to instability in their own country which was wracked by war and natural disasters. South Sudan had the highest percentage of its total population forcibly displaced. Aid agencies had warned that the returnees could overwhelm already struggling communities.

Somalia saw a thirty nine percent increase in forced displacement due to conflict bringing the total numbers to more than 5.1 million in a country of eighteen million people.

As the Somalia federal and state governments continued to lead an offensive against al Shabab, the violent extremist group, an increase in violence against civilians continued. This was expected to further drive-up levels of Somali refugees. The scale of displacement in Somalia was accentuated when environmental impacts were considered. Somalia had experienced the worst drought in forty years which caused crop failures year after year and killed millions of livestock.

A million people had been displaced from their homes in DRC because of violence linked to various non-state militia activity putting the number of displaced Congolese at over 7.1 million, a thirteen percent increase over the previous year.

Nigeria, Burkina Faso, Tigray, Ethiopia, told related stories.

It was no surprise to those that knew the region well, that new data revealed that without a fivefold increase in global aid to Africa, at least four million people would die of starvation over the next twelve months. The impossible goal of dramatically increasing aid loomed large, and time was running out.

It was not just the size of financial resources required it was also the logistics of delivering it. Few in the know believed a catastrophe could be averted.

As conditions worsened, young people in the most affected regions began to mass, desperate to flee their countries in search of a better life. Trafficking gangs exploited this desperation, increasing their operations. Significant numbers of refugees began arriving in Europe on small boats, far surpassing previous records.

The President held an emergency meeting with his inner circle, including Eleanor, to address this escalating crisis. The atmosphere was sombre as they grappled with the scale of the disaster.

"We're facing a humanitarian catastrophe of unprecedented proportions," the President began. "The combined global efforts aren't enough. We need a radical and novel approach alongside our international partners, and we need it now."

For many decades, the world had watched as the continent of Africa descended into chaos. The problems were manifold. Poor conditions in an excessively hot climate made agriculture on a scale to feed its own people an impossibility. A lack of investment in infrastructure and the basic requirements of economic growth was non-existent. Warlords dominated and nowhere was safe. Conflict was everywhere and there was no rule of law, often because there were no lawmakers, no legitimate government to steer the countries in question.

Corruption was rife, and murder on a scale was an everyday expectation. Despite everything populations grew exponentially.

Eleanor, ever the strategist, knew the impossibility of the task ahead. She proposed a multi-faceted plan, with the immediate need of feeding people as the priority. It was a complex scenario and there were no quick fix solutions.

The US, working alongside international aid agencies and allies, raised a record amount of cash to roll out feeding programmes throughout the region, all tempered by the complexities of local conflicts and wider wars. Delivering aid successfully in volume, and in a timely manner to be effective was critical, but often those in power within the region would put up physical and metaphorical barriers to inhibit the aid agencies work in fear they would lose power. They had no interest in the fact that their people were starving.

A part of the coordinated plan that would run parallel with the feeding programme was dealing with human trafficking. It was clear building infrastructure, stopping the wars, and establishing democratic government in the region had to take a back seat.

Within four months an international task force on human trafficking made considerable progress, coordinating efforts across countries to dismantle trafficking networks. Safe migration pathways began to emerge, providing controlled routes for some of those seeking to migrate. European countries slowly began to implement programmes to absorb greater numbers of migrants establishing local support infrastructures, but in truth it was merely a sticking plaster covering a gaping wound.

Slowly the situation did begin to stabilise as aid in its widest context started to arrive on the ground and distribution hubs were set up and managed. The immediate humanitarian response saved countless lives, and the long-term nature of the projects provided a base for future resilience. The influx of refugees into Europe was now better managed reducing the strain on host countries, and providing migrants with better prospects, but despite all the efforts, over a million people died on the continent of Africa in the following year and many more were displaced.

The scale of the crisis and the interventions undertaken were just the tip of the iceberg, the threat of future droughts, starvation and mass migration loomed large.

In addressing the press, the President conveyed a message of hope and determination. "We have made progress on the continent of Africa alongside our allies, but our work has only just begun. This crisis has shown us the power of international cooperation and the importance of acting with urgency and compassion. Together, we can build a future where no one must face famine."

Eleanor who helped draft the release knew they were hollow words. History was littered with interventions such as this garnering international support and action when the spotlight was turned on, but the moment the light went out the region returned to status quo. Conflicts raged, never ending wars decimated the countries in question and people on a scale died whether through brutality or starvation.

As the President's second term began to define itself, the pressure on the White House intensified. One disaster after another demanded attention, from natural calamities to geopolitical crises. The ongoing humanitarian crisis in Africa remained a critical issue, but the European Union's now tepid response and resistance to welcoming migrants added to the President's frustrations. Complicating matters further was the situation on the U.S.-Mexico border, where a new surge of migrants posed its own set of challenges, requiring careful navigation to avoid domestic and international fallout.

The President expressed his frustration during a high-level meeting with his inner circle, which included Eleanor, the Secretary of State, the National Security Adviser, and other senior advisers.

"The EU's response to the African crisis is unacceptable," he began. "They're refusing to take in more migrants, even as thousands risk their lives to reach their shores. This lack of action is exacerbating the situation and undermining our collective efforts."

Eleanor nodded in agreement. "We need to find a way to address this without alienating our European allies. Criticising them publicly could backfire and make cooperation even harder."

The Secretary of State commented. "We should initiate private discussions with key EU leaders. We need to emphasise the humanitarian aspects and the long-term benefits of a coordinated response. We can also offer to share some of the burden, showing solidarity and leadership."

Simultaneously, the President was grappling with a similar situation at the Mexican border. The surge of migrants required immediate and humane solutions that balanced security concerns with compassion. He knew instructing the military to 'shoot at will' was not the most diplomatic answer to the problem.

Eleanor briefly outlined an immediate action plan, acknowledging such initiatives take time:

1. Enhanced Border Security and Processing: Increase resources for border security while ensuring that processing centres are adequately staffed and equipped to manage the influx humanely and efficiently. This included expanding asylum processing capabilities and improving conditions at detention centres.
2. Regional Cooperation: Strengthen cooperation with Mexico and Central American countries to address the root causes of migration. This involved increasing aid and development projects to improve economic conditions, reduce violence, and enhance stability in the region.
3. Legal Pathways: Expand legal pathways for migration, including temporary work programs and family reunification initiatives. This would help reduce the pressure on the border by providing migrants with safe and legal alternatives.

The President and Eleanor set up a series online private meetings with key EU leaders. They emphasised the urgency of the crisis in Africa and the need for a united response. They also highlighted the connection of global migration issues, pointing out that instability in one region could have far-reaching impacts elsewhere. They all knew that climate change was playing a significant part in creating the arid conditions making it impossible for indigenous populations to feed themselves. Without water, cattle died, and crops withered, and soon, there would be little chance of human beings surviving in such scorching conditions.

History was littered with examples of human hardship that eventually lead to conflict, and the continent of Africa was no stranger to this dynamic.

"We understand the challenges you're facing," the President told the EU leaders. "But turning away those in desperate need isn't a solution. We must work together to find sustainable ways to address this crisis. The United States is ready to do its part, but we need your cooperation."

Eleanor had drafted the Presidents words knowing that his demands upon the EU were not mirrored by his thoughts and desired actions on the Mexican border, but he delivered his wise words anyway.

Eleanor proposed a joint task force to develop a coordinated response plan. This task force would focus on enhancing humanitarian aid, improving conditions for migrants, and creating long-term strategies for stability in Africa identifying the root causes of poverty and conflict. Of course, the answers were already known.

To build momentum and foster a global response, the President called for an international summit on migration and humanitarian aid.

Held in Geneva, the summit aimed to bring together leaders from around the world, including the EU, African nations, and other key stakeholders.

In his opening address, the President highlighted the broad nature of the crises. "Migration is a global challenge that requires a global response. We must work together to address the immediate needs of those suffering while also tackling the root causes of displacement. This is not just a moral imperative but a strategic necessity."

At home, the President implemented the proposed measures in Eleanor's plan to address the situation at the Mexican border. The enhanced border security and processing capabilities helped manage the influx more humanely, while regional cooperation efforts began to show promise in addressing the root causes of migration. Of course, climate change was the key contributor and would have far reaching effects long into the future. The world had pledged to reduce climate emissions, but progress was far too slow with governments mindful of economic constraints and opposition in some quarters for radical action.

The expansion of legal pathways for migration also helped reduce the pressure on the border, providing migrants with safer and more orderly options but progress was laboured.

The President, in a speech to the nation, acknowledged the difficulties but expressed hope for the future. "We are facing unprecedented challenges, but we are also making unprecedented efforts. By working together, both at home and abroad, we can build a more compassionate and stable world. This journey is long, but with perseverance and unity, we will have influence."

The intense focus on the African humanitarian crisis had inadvertently led the White House to shift attention away from other global conflicts, including those in Ukraine, the Gaza Strip, and Taiwan. Recent summits, intended to foster dialogue and cooperation, had become little more than talking shops, with scant progress visible on the ground.

The resurgence of military aggression by North Korea and Russia further complicated the situation. Recognising the need for a comprehensive review, the President called his inner circle to Camp David to brainstorm new strategies for addressing the conflicts.

At Camp David, the President, Eleanor, the Secretary of State, the National Security Adviser, and other key advisers gathered to reassess their approach to the world's most pressing conflicts. The goal was to review existing and develop new actionable strategies that could bring about real change.

The President opened the discussion by addressing the situation in Ukraine. Russian military aggression had intensified, and diplomatic efforts were hitting a wall. There seemed little hope that Russia would withdraw from the territory, quite the reverse they had ramped up their attacks on key targets in Ukraine and hundreds of innocent people had been killed.

The National Security Adviser commented "Our sanctions haven't deterred Russia as much as we hoped.

We need to rethink our strategy and perhaps involve more direct support for Ukraine."

Eleanor added. "We should increase our support for Ukraine not only militarily but also economically and diplomatically. This means more defensive aid, intelligence sharing, and economic assistance to help them withstand Russian pressure."

The Secretary of State commented. "A renewed diplomatic push is essential. We should engage more actively with our European allies to present a united front and consider involving neutral mediators to explore potential negotiations."

The discussions were wide ranging, and intelligence provided an accurate foundation to formulate future actions.

The President summed up the discussions, emphasising the need for a coordinated and multifaceted approach to these global challenges. "We cannot afford to ignore any of these conflicts. Our strategies must combine military readiness with robust diplomacy and economic support. The world looks to us for leadership." He added as an aside. "If we could have orchestrated the removal of the Russian President months ago the world would be a better place."

The Camp David summit concluded with a renewed sense of purpose and a detailed action plan for each conflict. The President and his team committed to executing these strategies with urgency aiming to restore stability where possible and promote peace in these troubled regions. It was acknowledged by everyone that little could be achieved without the support and commitment of allies.

The next steps involved immediate diplomacy, enhanced aid packages, and strategic military deployments. The President addressed the nation, reaffirming his administration's commitment to global stability and humanitarian values.

CHAPTER SIXTEEN

ELEANOR'S INTIMATE MOMENTS WITH THE PRESIDENT

It was close to 8.00 pm on a Tuesday evening. The President was leaving the Oval Office to return to his Presidential Private Quarters. Eleanor had left her office heading for home when the two met in a corridor. After exchanging pleasantries, the President asked Eleanor if she would like to have supper with him. Her reaction was to politely decline his invitation. She knew how important it was to maintain a professional distance between her and the President. The President looked disappointed and jokingly threatened to issue an 'Executive Order' if she refused. Eleanor smiled wryly. She knew by agreeing to his 'order' she would be compromising her professional standards but agreed anyway. They walked silently to the President's luxury apartment and was greeted by Edward Lyons - the President's Butler-Chef. "Mr President, Madame. Is it two for supper this evening, sir? Edward, like Eleanor was a Brit and their accent was not missed on the President. "So, two Brits infiltrating the Oval Office." They all smiled.

The President suggested Eleanor relax, they would not be talking about Africa, the Middle East, Russia, or China, or indeed the domestic agenda. Their easy conversation prior to supper established some odd coincidences. They were both 46 years of age, born only a few days apart. He was the youngest US President in history to take office. She was born in London. Her father a British diplomat, her mother an American surgeon. She was educated at Cambridge University gaining a double first in psychiatry and politics before moving to Washington to set up private practice. He was born in Boston and educated at Harvard and Yale majoring in Economics and Politics. He established his own software business eventually selling the asset for millions of dollars. His father was a surgeon, and his mother had a high-ranking job in government.

Eleanor, ever the professional, was keen to monitor the President's conversational content, his mannerisms and charm to try and discern if there was anything new, she could discover about his personality traits. She was aware of his infidelities.

He was an attractive and powerful man and would have found it easy to establish romantic relationships. He had presence, and honed communication skills. He had no idea she was weighing him up, but even if had suspected anything it didn't show, he was relaxed and open. They discovered they both had a passion for sailing and skiing although both admitted they had never had the time to enjoy either fully. Eleanor had never married but had been involved in a few relationships over the years, but her work had always taken precedence.

As the evening progressed, the atmosphere became more informal. The President and Eleanor delved deeper into their personal histories, sharing anecdotes about their families and friends. The President recounted his adventurous college days, filled with debates and late-night strategy sessions and drinking, while Eleanor shared stories of her international upbringing, navigating diverse cultures and expectations.

Edward Lyons, the ever-attentive butler-chef, served a meticulously prepared meal. The food was exquisite, but it was the company that made the meal memorable for both of them.

Eleanor found herself genuinely enjoying the President's company. Despite her initial reservations, she appreciated his wit, intelligence, and the subtle vulnerabilities he occasionally let slip. The President, on his part, seemed to relish the rare opportunity to unwind and engage in a conversation that wasn't strictly bound by political constraints or agendas, and with an attractive and intelligent woman.

After dinner, they talked about their hopes and fears, their successes, and regrets. It was a rare and candid exchange, the kind that both had missed in their busy, high-pressure lives.

As the evening ended, the President thanked Eleanor for her company and expressed how much he valued their time together. Eleanor, feeling a mix of emotions, realised that the evening had been a turning point. She had seen a different side of the President, one that was more human and less encumbered by the weight of his office.

Walking back to her car, she reflected on the night's events. She knew the importance of maintaining professional boundaries, but she also appreciated the value of genuine human connection, even in the highest corridors of power. As she drove home, she couldn't help but feel a sense of anticipation about what the future might hold, both professionally and personally.

The next day, as Eleanor returned to her routine, she reflected on the evening with the President. He too, seemed more at ease and focused, rejuvenated by genuine human contact and conversation, rather than the subservient exchanges he endured every day as one does in high office. It was a reminder that behind the titles and responsibilities, they were both just people trying to navigate the complexities of their lives.

In the days that followed, their professional interactions remained as focused and respectful as ever, but there was an unspoken understanding between them. They had shared a moment of genuine connection, one that, while not altering their professional dynamics, added a layer of mutual respect and empathy to their relationship

As days turned into weeks, Eleanor and the President continued to cross paths frequently, their professional relationship fortified by the unspoken bond they had forged during that evening. Each encounter was underscored by a new level of ease and mutual respect. They often exchanged glances and subtle smiles during meetings, small gestures that spoke volumes without uttering a word.

One Friday afternoon, the President, looking more relaxed than usual, called Eleanor into the Oval Office. "Eleanor," he began, "I wanted to thank you again for that evening. It was refreshing to talk about something other than politics."

Eleanor nodded, a warm smile on her face.

The President leaned back in his chair, a thoughtful expression on his face. "You know, I've been thinking a lot about balance, how to better manage the demands of this job while not losing sight of who I am outside of it. Your perspective has been invaluable."

Eleanor appreciated his comment. "It's important we often get so caught up in our roles that we forget to take care of ourselves."

Their conversation was interrupted by a knock on the door.

It was the Chief of Staff, with a stack of files needing the President's immediate attention. Eleanor excused herself, leaving the President to his work, but she couldn't shake the feeling that their connection was deepening, evolving beyond mere professional acquaintance.

Over the next few months, their interactions took on a more collaborative tone. Eleanor found herself being consulted on a wider array of issues; her insights valued in policy discussions that extended beyond her usual remit. She was becoming a trusted confidante; someone the President could rely on for both professional advice and personal support.

One evening, as Eleanor was leaving her office, she received a call from the President. "Eleanor, are you free to join me for a walk?" he asked. The request was unexpected but welcome. She agreed, curious about what was on his mind.

They met in the Rose Garden, the evening air cool and fragrant. The President seemed thoughtful. They walked in silence for a while before he spoke.

"Eleanor, I've been thinking about legacy. About what kind of President I want to be remembered for. There's so much pressure to make the right decisions, to please everyone. Sometimes, it feels overwhelming."

Eleanor listened; after all this was her area of expertise. "Legacy is important, but so is authenticity. People will remember you not just for your policies, but for who you are as a person. It's okay to be vulnerable, to show your human side. It doesn't make you any less of a leader."

The President nodded, taking in her words. "You're right. I've been so focused on being the perfect President that I've forgotten to just be myself."

They continued their walk, the conversation flowing naturally. Eleanor felt a deep sense of fulfilment, knowing that she was making a difference not just through her professional expertise but also through her ability to connect on a human level.

As they went their separate ways, the President thanked her once again. "You've given me a lot to think about, Eleanor. I appreciate your honesty and your friendship."

Eleanor smiled, feeling a profound sense of purpose. "Anytime, Mr. President. Remember, you're not alone in this."

From that night on, their bond only strengthened. Eleanor's presence became a source of stability for the President, a reminder that even the most powerful individuals need a confidante, someone who sees beyond the title and into the person behind it. And in Eleanor, the President had found exactly that.

Days later, the President once again invited Eleanor for supper. Although she had warm feelings for The President, she was extremely aware that she had branded him a psychopath, her professional instincts remained unchanged and wondered if it were wise to dine with him for a second time. Despite knowing about his past relationships and his ongoing marriage, she agreed.

As she walked to the President's private quarters, Eleanor couldn't help but feel a mix of excitement and apprehension. She was acutely aware of the potential consequences of blurring the lines between professional and personal boundaries, yet her curiosity and attraction overpowered her reservations.

Edward Lyons greeted her at the door with his usual impeccable manners. "Good evening, Madame. The President is waiting for you in the dining room."

Eleanor entered to find the President standing by the window, looking out over the city. He turned and smiled warmly when he saw her. "Eleanor, thank you for coming. It's been a long week, and I could use the company."

They sat down to a beautifully set table, the ambiance both intimate and relaxed. Edward had outdone himself once again.

As they ate, their conversation flowed effortlessly. They discussed their latest work challenges, shared amusing anecdotes, and found common ground in their shared interests. Eleanor noticed how the President's eyes lit up when he talked about policy ideas or recounted stories from his past. Despite the power and responsibility, he carried, there was a genuine warmth to him that she found increasingly appealing.

After supper, they moved to a more comfortable seating area. The President poured them both a glass of wine, and they settled into a deeper conversation. Eleanor found herself opening up about other aspects of her life she had not told him about, her struggles, and her aspirations in a way she hadn't with anyone else.

"I never imagined I'd end up here, in this position," the President admitted, his tone reflective. "Sometimes, I wonder what my life would have been like if I'd stayed in business."

Eleanor nodded, understanding the weight of his words. "We all have those moments of doubt, wondering about the 'what ifs.' But you're here for a reason, making a difference in ways you might not even realise."

The President looked at her. "And you, Eleanor? Have you ever wondered what your life would be like if you'd chosen a different path?"

Eleanor paused, contemplating her response. "Sometimes. But I believe every experience, every choice, has led me to where I am today. And despite the challenges, I wouldn't change a thing." There was a moment of silence, charged with unspoken emotions.

The President reached out, gently taking her hand. "I'm glad you're here, Eleanor. Your presence means more to me than you know."

Eleanor's heart raced. She knew she was treading dangerous waters, but the connection she felt with the President was undeniable. She squeezed his hand lightly, a silent acknowledgment of the bond they shared.

As the evening ended, the President walked Eleanor to the door. "Thank you for another wonderful evening," he said softly. "I hope we can do this again soon."

Eleanor smiled, "I'd like that, Mr. President."

As she left, Eleanor couldn't shake the feeling that she was on the brink of something significant. The attraction she felt for the President was undeniable, but so were the risks. She knew she had to tread carefully, balancing her professional integrity with the growing personal connection she couldn't ignore.

The days that followed were a blur of meetings and official duties, but the memory of that evening lingered in Eleanor's mind. She found herself looking forward to their next encounter. The President, too, seemed more energised and focused, their private conversations providing a respite from the relentless demands of his role.

In the high-stakes world they inhabited, their connection was a rare and precious thing. And while the future remained uncertain, one thing was clear: their bond was deepening, and neither was willing to let it go.

Aside from official meetings, Eleanor and the President often passed each other in the corridors of the White House, exchanging affectionate smiles that spoke volumes. Eleanor was becoming increasingly aware that her intense focus on work was being diluted by her growing affection for the President. She found herself eagerly anticipating his next supper invitation.

One evening, as she was concluding her work for the day, her phone pinged with a message. It was from the President:

"Are you free for supper tonight? I could use some good company."

Eleanor's heart skipped a beat. She quickly replied, accepting the invitation. As she made her way to the President's private quarters, she felt a mix of excitement and apprehension.

Edward Lyons greeted her at the door with a warm smile. "Good evening, Madame. The President is expecting you."

Eleanor entered to find the President waiting in the living room, a bottle of wine and two glasses on the table. "Eleanor, it's good to see you," he said, his smile genuine and welcoming. They settled into conversation, appreciating the others company.

Edward served a delicious meal; the food was excellent. As they talked, Eleanor relaxed, the stresses of the day disappearing from her mind.

"Eleanor, I've been thinking a lot about our conversations," The President said. "You have a way of making me see things differently, more clearly."

Eleanor smiled. "I'm glad I can help, Mr. President. You've given me a lot to think about too."

"You mean a lot to me, Eleanor. More than I can express."

The intensity of his gaze, the sincerity in his voice, left no doubt about his feelings. She knew she was at a crossroads, where professional boundaries and personal desires collided.

"Mr. President," she began, her voice trembling slightly, "this connection we have... it's complicated. But I can't deny how much it means to me."

He nodded, understanding the unspoken implications of her words. "I know, Eleanor. But sometimes, the most meaningful things in life are the most complicated."

They sat in silence for a moment, then, with a gentle squeeze of her hand, the President spoke. "Whatever happens, I want you to know that I'm grateful for your presence in my life."

Eleanor felt tears welling up in corners of her eyes. "And I'm grateful for yours, Mr. President."

As the evening ended, the President walked Eleanor to the door. "Goodnight, Eleanor. I look forward to our next supper."

"Goodnight, Mr. President,"

The days that followed were marked by their usual professional interactions, but the undercurrent of their personal connection remained. Each passing smile, each shared glance, was a reminder of the evening they had spent together and the unspoken promise of more to come.

Weeks later, Eleanor received a text message from the President that made her smile.

"Eleanor, I haven't seen you for a while. I know it's a lot to ask, but would you like to go sailing with me next weekend? I think it's about time we both renewed our passion!"

Eleanor read the message several times, a smile spreading across her face. She felt a mix of excitement and trepidation. The idea of spending an entire weekend with the President, away from the confines of the White House, was both thrilling and daunting. After a moment of contemplation, she replied:

"I would love to go sailing with you, Mr. President. It sounds like the perfect way to unwind. Count me in!"

The following Friday, Eleanor packed a small bag and made her way to the marina, where the President's yacht was docked. She had no idea whether he owned the craft or whether it was a perk of the job, but there it was, sleek, elegant, and waiting for wind to hit its sails. The President was on deck, looking relaxed and casual.

"Eleanor! Welcome aboard," he greeted her with a warm smile.

"Thank you, Mr. President," she replied, returning his smile. "This is beautiful."

"Please, you must call me Daniel when we're out here," he said. "This weekend is about enjoying ourselves and leaving titles behind."

Eleanor nodded, appreciating the informality.

The day was filled with laughter and light-hearted conversation. They shared stories about their childhoods, their dreams, and the journeys that had led them to where they were now. The President's passion for sailing was evident, and Eleanor found herself captivated by his enthusiasm and his skill. She too took the helm and had remembered more than she had forgotten about the art of sailing.

As the sun began to set, casting a golden glow over the water, they anchored in a secluded cove. The President prepared a simple but delicious meal. They ate on deck.

"Thank you for coming, Eleanor," he said as they finished their meal. "I've missed our conversations."

"I've missed them too," she admitted. "This was a wonderful idea."

Later, the President turned to her, his expression serious. "Eleanor, there's something I need to say. Our time together has meant a lot to me. I know the situation is complicated, but I want you to know that my feelings for you are real."

Eleanor felt a mix of high emotion and fear. "I feel the same way," she confessed. "But we have to be careful. The stakes are high especially for you."

"I know," he said softly. "But I believe we can find a way to make this work, if we're both willing to try."

They sat in silence for a while, the weight of their words hanging in the air. The connection between them was undeniable, but so were the challenges they faced.

As the night grew cooler, they moved below deck. The President prepared a small bed for Eleanor, ensuring she was comfortable.

"Goodnight, Eleanor, sleep well."

The next morning, they awoke to the sound of seagulls and the gentle rocking of the boat as the waves lapped its side. After a leisurely breakfast, they spent the day exploring the coastline, stopping to swim in the clear, blue waters and basked in the sun. Eleanor expected security to be ever-present around the President and questioned him. "I'm surprised not to see a flotilla of security following our every move." The President smiled. "It's not easy to escape them, but every now and then I'm allowed some privacy."

By the end of the weekend, Eleanor felt the time away had given her renewed perspective. She knew despite the risks and the President's complicated personal life; she was willing to explore the connection she shared with him.

As they sailed back to the marina, the President turned to her. "Thank you for this weekend, Eleanor. It was exactly what I needed." Immediately, security was there surrounding the President as he disembarked.

"Me too," she replied. "Let's not wait too long before we do this again." They returned to their respective routines, but the bond between them was stronger than ever.

Eleanor's friendship with the President was constantly on her mind, and she worried it was diminishing her focus on her work. Despite the personal distractions, there was much to do as international matters continued to challenge the White House. She tried to immerse herself in her duties, but her thoughts frequently drifted to the President and their recent time together.

It was a Friday morning, and everything seemed eerily quiet as she worked in her office. The stillness was suddenly shattered by the blaring of the evacuation alarm. Eleanor joined the stream of people heading towards the designated assembly area on the lawns. There was no panic, everyone was regularly drilled on procedure.

Outside, the atmosphere was tense. Security personnel were everywhere, guiding people to safety and scanning the perimeter with steely vigilance. Eleanor spotted the President among the crowd; Secret Service agents quickly surrounded him.

"Stay calm, everyone. Follow instructions," a voice boomed over the loudspeakers.

The security services had been alerted to intruders, there was a belief that a terrorist attack on the White House was underway, with the aim of assassinating the President.

From her position on the lawn, Eleanor could see agents moving systematically through the building. She glanced around, seeking any sign of immediate danger, but everything seemed under control.

After what felt like an age, a senior security officer approached the President and his inner circle. "Mr. President, we've swept the premises. No intruders found. It appears to have been a false alarm, but we will remain on high alert until we are absolutely certain."

The collective sigh of relief was almost audible.

Eventually, the White House teams returned to their offices. The rest of the day passed in a blur of meetings and briefings. That evening, as she reflected on the day's events, she received another text message from the President:

"Thank you for your support today. Dinner soon?"

Eleanor smiled. She replied immediately.

"Absolutely, when it's right for you!"

Eleanor's concern grew as her affection for the President deepened. She had fallen in love, but she knew it was impossible to establish anything remotely resembling a normal relationship with him.

He was married, had a mistress and two children, and, in her professional opinion, he was a psychopath. The complexity and ethical dilemmas of their situation weighed heavily on her mind.

Realising she needed to regain control over her life and career, Eleanor made a difficult decision: she would no longer see the President socially. She would refocus her attention on her job, where she was most needed.

That evening, Eleanor sat at her desk, she picked up her phone and composed a message to the President:

'Mr. President, I deeply value our friendship and the moments we've shared. However, it is best for both of us if I focus solely on my professional duties from now on. I hope you understand.'

The next couple of days were challenging. The international matters demanding her attention provided a welcome distraction from her personal turmoil. She had not had a response from the President.

On day three, her phone pinged with a message from the President:

'I respect your decision, Eleanor, but I hope you know how much your friendship means to me. Take care.'

She felt sadness but also a sense of relief.

The White House was bustling with activity as always, and Eleanor found herself immersed in pressing issues involving Africa, the Middle East, Russia, and China. Her expertise and dedication were crucial in navigating these complex situations, and she knew she couldn't afford any distractions.

Despite her determination, Eleanor couldn't completely shut off her feelings. She still cared deeply for the President and worried about him, but she reminded herself of the reasons behind her decision. The boundaries she had set were necessary, even if they were painful.

Over time, Eleanor noticed a change in herself. Her focus returned, and her work flourished. She became more efficient, more driven, and more respected among her colleagues. The President, too, seemed to respect her decision, maintaining a professional distance while still valuing her input and advice.

The Oval Office was once again at the centre of a major crisis. Illegal drug imports had reached an all-time high, overwhelming the DEA and putting immense strain on law enforcement. Tens of millions of Americans were thought to be addicted to narcotics, and the ripple effects were devastating for societal cohesion, the economy, healthcare systems, and community safety. Gun crimes linked directly to the drug war were claiming dozens of lives each week. Congress demanded the President take decisive action.

Eleanor and the top team were briefed on the situation with growing concern. The drug epidemic was a multifaceted issue that developed over decades and there was no quick fix. Whatever strategy was adopted to arrest the situation would take hundreds of billions of dollars and years to have an impact. Drugs were an ever-present part of everyday life and communities were both devastated by addiction but also, in a perverse way, reliant upon the drug trade for survival.

In a high-level meeting in the Oval Office, the President gathered his top advisers, including Eleanor, to discuss a way forward.

"Mr. President," began the Secretary of Homeland Security, "the DEA is stretched to the limit. We need to allocate significantly more resources in manpower and detection regimes and improve coordination with local law enforcement agencies."

The Secretary of Health and Human Services commented, "We must also address the root causes of addiction. This means expanding access to mental health services and addiction treatment programmes. To have a real impact, Mr President, it will cost hundreds of billions and take years to have real effect. There is no quick fix."

Eleanor listened carefully, taking notes. She knew that a successful strategy would require a balance of enforcement, prevention, and treatment.

"Mr. President, as has already been said, this is a major societal problem in this and other countries around the world, and all indicators suggest drug addiction is uncontrollable. If we are serious about containing the problem, because I believe we will never control or eradicate illegal drug use, we must adopt an intelligent strategy that commits people and resources only in those areas where we can expect measurable results. We must strengthen our borders and enhance intelligence operations to disrupt the drug supply chains. Simultaneously, we should invest in community programmes that focus on prevention and provide community support for those struggling with addiction. This is not just a law enforcement issue; it's a public health crisis that threatens the very fabric of society."

The President agreed. "Eleanor, your insights are invaluable. We need a realistic plan and budget to take to Congress. I would like you to spearhead this project calling on whatever resources you need."

Eleanor smiled but knew just how demanding this single project would be on her time, and with everything else on her desk that also demanded her attention it would not be easy. "Thank you, Mr President. I will start the project immediately."

As the plan took shape, the President prepared to address the nation. He knew the American people were looking to him for leadership and reassurance.

"My fellow Americans," he began, "our nation is facing an unprecedented crisis. The illegal drug trade is wreaking havoc on our communities, our economy, and our healthcare system. We are losing too many lives to addiction and violence.

Today, I am announcing a comprehensive plan to combat this epidemic. We will strengthen our borders, enhance law enforcement efforts, and expand access to treatment and prevention programmes. This is a battle we cannot afford to lose, and together, we must bring about lasting change so our people can live in an environment where the fear of drugs decimating our communities ends. It will take considerable time and effort and will cost billions of taxpayers' dollars to put right, but this administration is determined to be effective."

The response was immediate. The media buzzed with headlines equally balanced between optimism and pessimism, polls suggested public opinion was cautiously optimistic.

In the weeks that followed, Eleanor tried to balance the demands of her 'in tray' but focused her attention on this project as a priority.

As the months passed, progress was evident. Drug seizures increased, treatment programmes expanded, and public awareness campaigns began to shift perceptions about addiction.

The implementation of the President's comprehensive plan to combat the drug epidemic was in full swing. Eleanor's dedication and expertise had positioned her as a key player in the effort, and she found herself busier than ever. The crisis demanded constant vigilance, and the weight of responsibility was immense. As she had made clear in the Oval Office the most the administration could hope to do was manage the illegal drug trade, there was no prospect of resolving it.

CHAPTER SEVENTEEN

DRUG EPIDEMIC OUT OF CONTROL

One evening, as Eleanor was reviewing reports in her office, there was a knock on her door. It was the President.

"Do you have a moment?" he asked.

"Of course, Mr. President," she replied, setting aside her work.

He took a seat across from her. "I wanted to thank you for your extraordinary work on the drug project. You're doing a fabulous job, Eleanor, and your initiatives are having an impact."

Eleanor felt a mixture of pride and sadness. She had managed to maintain her professional boundaries, but her feelings for the President were never far from her thoughts. "Thank you, Mr. President. It's a team effort, and we still have a long way to go."

He nodded. "I know. But I'm confident that we're on the right path. Your commitment has been a source of strength for me."

They shared a brief, silent moment of understanding before the President stood up to leave. "Keep up the excellent work, Eleanor. We need you."

Over time intelligence data showed tangible results. Drug seizures at the border increased significantly, and intelligence operations successfully dismantled several major trafficking networks. Public health initiatives started to gain traction, with more people accessing addiction treatment and mental health services. The media reported on these successes, and public confidence grew.

The fight against the drug epidemic was complex and multifaceted, and setbacks were inevitable. One particularly challenging day, Eleanor received an urgent call from the Secretary of Homeland Security.

A major drug cartel had retaliated against law enforcement leading to a violent confrontation that resulted in multiple DEA fatalities. The situation was dire.

Eleanor organised an emergency meeting in the Situation Room to formulate a response and issue a statement supporting the DEA in their work.

"Mr. President, we need to escalate our efforts," the Secretary of Homeland Security urged. "This attack shows that the cartels are willing to go to extreme lengths to protect their operations."

The President turned to Eleanor. "What's your assessment?"

"We do need to increase our support for local law enforcement and provide additional resources for intelligence operations, especially the DEA," Eleanor said. "At the same time, we must continue to address the root causes of addiction to reduce demand, but Mr President we need to be realistic. The country cannot afford the kind of draconian measures we would need to implement to make a significant difference in our communities the electorate are expecting. There are so many moving parts, so many variables, so much we cannot control." She knew she was offering a sombre message, but it had to be said.

The President nodded. "I understand and thank you for your honesty. Let's ensure that with the resources we have that we're doing everything possible to protect our people and support those on the front lines of this fight. I will seek additional resources from Congress, let's see where that takes us."

Increased funding for local law enforcement, enhanced protection for the DEA, and intensified efforts to track and dismantle cartel networks was agreed. Public health initiatives were expanded, with additional resources allocated to prevention and treatment programmes, but in truth Eleanor and the inner circle including the President knew it would only scratch the surface of this decades long deep-rooted problem. Drug trafficking and addiction were here to stay irrespective of how much was invested to curtail it. The future for all developed nations around the world looked bleak.

Eleanor and her team commissioned a report on the status and future predictions for the illegal drug trade. They knew there was no permanent solution that would eradicate drugs from the streets, but Eleanor in particular, did not believe the administration had enough information and hard data about the true status of the problem.

The report took far more time than anticipated and only confirmed what was already believed to be the case, drug addiction was endemic and impossible to control. Significant financial investments amounting to one hundred billion dollars a year was required and on a recurring basis, not to bring an end to the problem, but to manage the malignant effect it was having on society and avoid anarchy. It made for grim reading. Eleanor poured over the document line for line as others, including the President, only read the key headlines.

The 125- page report concluded:

'There are lessons to be learned from European countries like Switzerland and the Netherlands. These countries broke with established paradigms and successfully tackled the heroin- and HIV-crisis of the 1990s by implementing heroin-assisted treatment as a novel and effective treatment regimen. These strategies to improve treatment are needed in North America and novel approaches like fentanyl-assisted treatment have already been proposed but are far from being evaluated and implemented

Mental health experts, particularly psychiatrists, need to step up and follow a comprehensive and integrated approach to addressing the opioid overdose crisis. The importance of the mental health care system is rooted in its capacity to address the co-occurrence of mental illness and substance use disorders, provide access to substance use treatment, integrate mental health and substance use services, and understand the psychological and social factors contributing to substance use disorders. Treatment barriers like waiting lists and long distances to the nearest treatment provider need to be overcome. Advocating for an expanded access to evidence-based medications is a key place to start. An effective response therefore requires the individual efforts of psychiatrists, as well as a system change, focused around integrating mental health care, social services, and counselling.

The current North American system of interventional silos between specialities must be abandoned to be able to respond to future drug market shifts and their potentially detrimental public health impact. All health care professionals must be empowered when treating patients with opioid use disorder, no matter their specialisation. This should include specialty-appropriate education and training for proper referral or management of patients. Such system-wide changes should be orchestrated by psychiatrists, other mental health professionals, and most importantly, patients and their families. Ending or controlling drug addiction in the USA and around the world is not a plausible objective. The focus must be on managing the crisis and its consumption trends providing a comprehensive support structure for addicts across a spectrum of need to contain rather than cure the problem. Failure to do so would risk societal breakdown on a scale unimaginable and anarchy would prevail on our streets.'

It was plain to Eleanor at least, that the recommendations of the report should be adopted, with Congress digging much deeper into the coffers to fund a recurring annual budget of around $100 billion, rather than the current $40 billion, which according to the report authors was being spent unwisely.

The President and his key advisers, who hadn't read the report in detail, railed against Eleanor's recommendation. The President commented "Reports come and go; we need to maintain our current expenditure and monitor progress more closely."

Those in the room nodded in support. The report was rejected. The war on drugs would continue to under-perform, as the day anarchy reached the streets drew closer.

Months of meticulous planning had prepared the President for a state visit to Canada. Both the US and Canada worked in harmony across many government departments, consistently maintaining their close relationship. The President eagerly anticipated his visit, with a comprehensive agenda to discuss the most pressing issues, including the war on drugs. Recently, Canada had legalised certain drug use, a move that generated both support and criticism. Time would reveal whether this initiative would yield positive results.

Air Force One departed from Washington, D.C., bound for Ottawa. En route, the Security Services received alarming intelligence: Middle Eastern extremists were targeting the President's plane. A safe landing in an alternative location became an urgent necessity.

The President was quickly briefed on the potential threat by his chief of security. Throughout the President remained composed, understanding the gravity of the situation and the need for swift action.

Meanwhile, in the secure operations room at the Pentagon, military strategists and intelligence officers worked to determine the safest possible diversion route.

They quickly identified several potential landing sites within reach, each evaluated for its security protocols and readiness to manage an emergency landing of Air Force One.

The President's team coordinated with the Canadian government, who were immediately informed of the situation. Prime Minister Austin Graham expressed his concern and pledged full support, mobilising Canadian military and security forces to assist in ensuring the President's safety.

As Air Force One changed course, heading for a secure airbase in Maine, fighter jets were dispatched to escort the plane. The situation was tense, but the presence of the military jets provided a measure of reassurance.

Onboard, the President continued to work with his advisers, making necessary adjustments to his agenda and maintaining communication with Canadian officials to keep the planned visit on track. The war on drugs, trade agreements, and environmental policies were all pressing topics that he intended to discuss, and he was determined that this incident would not derail their progress.

Upon landing safely in Maine, the President and his team were swiftly escorted to a secure location. The intelligence community continued to monitor the threat, working with international allies to track down the extremists responsible.

The incident served as a stark reminder of the constant vigilance required and the importance of the strong US-Canada partnership. The state visit would proceed, albeit with heightened security measures, as both nations continued their collaboration on mutual interests and global challenges.

Two days later, Air Force One once again took off from Maine, heading for Ottawa after the Security Services had given clearance that the threat had subsided.

Within ten minutes of taking off, the unthinkable happened: the radar picked up a missile heading directly toward Air Force One. The crew sprang into action, alerting the President executing emergency protocols. The pilot initiated evasive manoeuvres, banking sharply to the left to avoid the incoming threat. The fighter jets, which had been escorting the plane since take-off, moved into offensive positions, ready to intercept the missile.

The President, secured in the most fortified section of the plane, remained calm, trusting in his security team. Communications with defence agencies were immediately established, and ground-based missile defence systems were activated in an attempt to neutralise the threat.

As the missile closed in, the fighter jets launched countermeasures. Flares filled the sky, creating a display of light and debris intended to confuse the missile's guidance systems.

The combined efforts of the fighter jets and ground-based defences finally paid off; the missile veered off course and exploded harmlessly in the sky, far away from Air Force One.

The immediate danger had passed, but the incident was a stark reminder of the ongoing threats faced by global leaders. Security Services continued to work around the clock, coordinating with international intelligence agencies to identify and apprehend those responsible for the attack.

Despite the harrowing experience, the President remained stoical. The flight continued to Ottawa. Upon arrival, the President was greeted by Prime Minister Graham, who expressed his relief at the President's safe arrival and reaffirmed the strength of the US-Canada alliance.

Following the closely guarded state visit, the President returned to Washington. Security Services, prioritising his safety, insisted that he be transported on a private jet rather than Air Force One. This change was intended to reduce the risk of detection and potential threats. The return journey passed without incident, allowing the President and his team a moment of relief after the tense events of the past few days.

Back in Washington, intelligence reports confirmed that the attack on Air Force One had been orchestrated by Iranian proxies. This revelation heightened tensions and prompted immediate action from the administration. The President convened a meeting with his national security advisers, the Secretary of Defence, and key intelligence officials to discuss the implications and formulate a response.

The situation demanded a measured yet firm approach. Diplomatic channels were engaged to address the threat directly with Iran. The Secretary of State made a public statement condemning the attack and calling for an international response to hold those responsible accountable. Behind the scenes, covert operations were launched to gather further intelligence and dismantle the network involved in the attack.

Simultaneously, the President worked with Congress to ensure that security protocols were reviewed and enhanced, not just for Air Force One but for all aspects of presidential travel and security. Additional funding was allocated to bolster counter-terrorism efforts and improve defensive capabilities.

In his address to the nation, the President reassured the public, emphasising the resilience and strength of the country in the face of such threats. He reiterated the importance of international cooperation in combating terrorism and reaffirmed the US commitment to working with allies like Canada to promote global security and stability.

Despite the gravity of the situation, the President remained focused on the broader agenda of his administration. The state visit to Canada had been productive, and the discussions on the war on drugs, trade agreements, and environmental policies continued to move forward. The incident had underscored the importance of vigilance but also demonstrated the effectiveness of international partnerships in addressing shared challenges.

In the weeks that followed, the President maintained a busy schedule, addressing both domestic and international issues with renewed determination. The administration's swift and decisive response to the attack reinforced the nation's determination, sending a clear message that the United States would not be intimidated and would continue to lead in the fight against global terrorism.

CHAPTER EIGHTEEN

PRESIDENTIAL SCANDAL ERUPTS

News broke that Peter Rainer, a wealthy businessman who had significantly funded the President's election campaign, had been arrested for major fraud. Rainer's finance company had allegedly conned millions of Americans out of their savings and investments. The revelation sent shockwaves through the country given Rainer's close relationship with the President, dating back to their university days, and extending into their professional lives. It was Rainer who had helped finance the President's software company before his foray into politics.

The media and Congress immediately demanded a thorough investigation to determine if the President was implicated in any way. The President addressed the nation, expressing his shock and disappointment over the allegations against Rainer. He emphasised his commitment to justice and transparency, stating unequivocally that he had no knowledge of or involvement in Rainer's fraudulent activities.

To ensure a fair and unbiased investigation, the President pledged full cooperation with the authorities. He ordered the release of all relevant communications and financial records related to his interactions with Rainer and his companies. Additionally, he appointed an independent counsel to oversee the investigation, aiming to maintain public trust and demonstrate his administration's integrity.

Congress launched a bipartisan committee to investigate the matter, examining the extent of Rainer's fraud and any potential connections to the President. Hearings were held, and testimonies were taken from various individuals, including the President's associates and campaign staff.

The investigation scrutinised the financial transactions between Rainer's finance company and the President's election campaign, as well as their historical business dealings.

As the investigation progressed, it became clear that while the President had a long-standing personal and professional relationship with Rainer, there appeared to be no evidence to suggest that he had been aware of or involved in the fraudulent activities.

Despite being cleared of any wrongdoing, the President acknowledged the gravity of the situation, and the betrayal felt by the American public. He announced new measures to increase transparency and oversight in campaign financing, aiming to prevent such occurrences in the future. The administration also launched initiatives to support those affected by the fraud, working with financial institutions to help victims recover their lost savings and investments.

The scandal, while a significant challenge, reinforced the President's claim to uphold the highest ethical standards in his administration. The episode served as a reminder of the importance of vigilance and accountability in public office, and the need for robust safeguards to protect the interests of the American people.

One early evening in Eleanor's office soon after the scandal had died down, the President called in to see her after dining with a foreign dignity. It was clear to Eleanor he had consumed a good deal of alcohol. In a bizarre conversation he admitted to her that he had been involved in the Rainer financial scandal and rejoiced in the fact he had got away with it.

Eleanor was left in a state of turmoil after the President's unexpected confession. As a trusted adviser and confidant, she understood the gravity of the situation and the potential fallout if this information became public. The President had admitted to profiting from Peter Rainer's investment firm as a consultant, earning hundreds of thousands of dollars, yet failing to declare this income. This revelation posed a significant ethical and legal dilemma. After the President left her office and returned to his Presidential quarters, she weighed up her options. She could counsel the President to voluntarily disclose this information to the authorities and the public. Coming clean might mitigate some of the damage and demonstrate a commitment to transparency and accountability.

However, this would certainly lead to intense media scrutiny, legal repercussions, and potential political fallout. She could contact a legal expert to understand the implications of the President's admission and explore the best course of action.

This would provide a clearer picture of the potential consequences and help formulate a strategy for addressing the issue. If Eleanor felt that the President would not take the necessary steps to rectify the situation, she would consider informing the appropriate authorities. This would ensure that the matter was investigated and addressed, but it would certainly end her relationship with the President and the White House. Or she could choose to keep the President's confession to herself. This would avoid immediate fallout, but it would weigh heavily on her conscience and could result in severe consequences if the information were to come out later through other means.

Eleanor's final decision would have profound implications, not just for her and the President, but for the entire administration and the country. She knew that integrity and the rule of law had to be her guiding principles.

After careful consideration, she decided to speak with the President again, emphasising the importance of transparency and the potential long-term benefits of coming forward voluntarily.

A meeting was arranged in his private quarters rather than the Oval Office where conversations were recorded. She felt anxious as she entered the room. "Mr President…" Before she could continue, he stopped her in her tracks. "Eleanor, please call me Daniel in here, there is no need for formality between us." He smiled warmly making it even more difficult for her to unfold her thoughts. She paused.

"Daniel. When you came into my office the other evening you admitted to me that you had been involved in the Rainer scandal and got away with it, and I was shocked. Shocked that you had been involved and also surprised you would confess to me knowing that I always adhere to the rules. You have placed me in an awkward position…" The President realising he had made a major mistake in confessing to her stopped her short. "Eleanor, I was only joking, you must have realised that." She looked at him. "I'm sorry I don't believe you.

Your confession was the truth, and you only told me because you were intoxicated at the time and wasn't thinking clearly. My advice to you is to consult with legal counsel.

You need a reputable attorney to navigate the legal ramifications and prepare for potential investigations, or prepare a public statement acknowledging the omission, explaining the context, and expressing a commitment to rectify the situation. Or finally, commit to full transparency and cooperation with any resulting investigations to rebuild public trust."

Eleanor stressed that while any of these options would be challenging, it was the most ethically sound path and would serve the best interests of the President, the administration, and the nation.

The President's face dropped as it listened to her. "But Eleanor, any of those options would end my Presidency and cause political chaos at a time when we need stability and strength in the White House. You cannot expect me to do this. Look, I have only confessed to you alone. The investigation cleared me, can't we let sleeping dogs…" She interrupted him. "No. That is unacceptable. I cannot be a part of this knowing what I know. You must follow my advice otherwise I will have no option but to speak the truth."

The President spoke softly looking Eleanor in the eyes. He would try again. "I fully understand the dilemma I have placed you in, it is all my fault, but I beg you, your President begs you, to let this lie. Please do not act upon the knowledge you have. You and I have built a strong friendship, more than a friendship. Is it too much for me to call in a favour, please."

Eleanor was not about to change her mind. They agreed she would do and say nothing giving the President time to consider the options she placed before him. Within 24 hours he would speak with her again.

Eleanor had a sleepless night and returned to the office to face a full in-tray of work, but her mind could only focus on the meeting with the President the previous evening wondering what his response would be later in the day.

The day ended in the office, but the President had not contacted her. Another two days passed, and she was worried that the President hadn't taken her seriously. She knew, ethically and morally, she could not sweep his confession under the carpet irrespective of the potential fallout.

The following day approaching 2.00 pm word came in from intelligence sources that a major explosion had taken place at the Pentagon and was thought to be a terrorist attack. Eleanor immediately called her top team together and arranged a meeting with the President in the Oval Office. This would be the first time she had seen The President since their discussion about the Rainer affair days earlier. She dreaded the encounter.

Just as they had assembled in the Oval Office awaiting the President to arrive, word came in that Security Services had discovered that the explosion had nothing to do with a terror attack but was due to an electrical failure and subsequent explosion. Eleanor stood down the assembled team just as The President arrived.

"What's the latest" he said. The Chief of Staff appraised the President who was visibly relieved and thanked everyone for assembling so quickly. He took the opportunity to ask Eleanor to stay behind.

After everyone had left The President sat on the edge of his desk and invited Eleanor to sit.

"I'm sorry I haven't got back to you since we spoke the other day, it's been tough these past few days. I have considered what you said, and I know you want me to confess about the Rainer stuff for reasons of transparency, but I just cannot do it. There is too much at stake. There are so many issues, critical issues on my desk right now, if I do as you ask the White House will be thrown into turmoil and we will appear weak on the international stage. We would risk pariah nations taking advantage and I just cannot allow that. I'm afraid, the decision is yours, Eleanor, turn me in and unleash catastrophic consequences or support me to do what I can to make our nation a better place for our people and for world order."

Eleanor listened intently knowing from the first words he uttered he was about to manipulate her. She could have written his script.

"Mr President…" He stopped her and smiled. "Call me Daniel." She ignored his words. "Mr President. You place me in an invidious position but as I explained to you the other evening I cannot turn a blind eye. If you are not prepared to do the right thing I will have to act. It is your choice Mr President."

He stared at her momentarily. "Then you must do what you must do, but I will vehemently deny anything you say. The investigation found no evidence, and you certainly have none other than an admission I made to you, so it would be your word against mine. Is this how you want this to continue, Eleanor? Can we not agree to stop this now?"

Eleanor left the room without uttering another word.

Overnight she had not slept. She was angry that the President tried to manipulate her, but even more, angry with herself for thinking he would do anything else.

She knew him well, she had fallen for him, even to the point of confessing to herself that she loved him, but all the time from a professional standpoint, as a renowned psychiatrist, she knew he suffered from psychopathy. He would do anything to stay in power irrespective of the damage he could do and the relationships he would shatter. She was now faced with a potentially life-changing if not life-threatening decision to 'tell all or say nothing' and wipe her mind clean of the President's confession.

She returned to her office exhausted the following morning ill-prepared for a day's work. As she opened some internal mail there was a hubbub of noise in the next office and she went to see what the fuss was all about.

It was out. The President had issued a personal statement, not drawn up by his advisers but prepared by himself. It was brief but had the potential to end his career in the White House. He admitted that he had been involved with Rainer and had accepted consulting fees from the firm which he was wrong to withhold from the investigating committee.

He had decided to consult with legal advisers immediately and began preparing for a public disclosure.

The President, after hearing Eleanor's advice, now recognised the seriousness of his situation. He understood that his failure to declare the earnings from Rainer's investment firm could not be ignored. Despite the potential personal and political fallout, he agreed to take the necessary steps to address the issue. He knew, whatever he said to Eleanor she would not back down.

The President arranged a confidential meeting with a reputable legal team specialising in political ethics and compliance. The attorneys outlined the potential legal repercussions, including violations of financial disclosure laws and conflicts of interest. They stressed the importance of voluntary disclosure to mitigate the severity of any penalties.

With the guidance of his legal team the President began drafting a full public statement. He aimed to be transparent, taking full responsibility for his oversight while providing context for his actions. The statement included an admission of failing to disclose his financial gains from consulting with the firm. An explanation of that consulting work and the reasons behind the omission, emphasising any unintentional actions. A pledge to rectify the situation, including amending financial disclosures and cooperating with any investigations.

Before making the public announcement, the President held a meeting with his senior advisers and key members of his administration including Eleanor. He explained the situation, his decision to disclose the information, and the steps he would be taking. This transparency was crucial to maintaining internal support and preparing the team for the potential fallout. Throughout his gaze was on Eleanor, not in an aggressive manner but in a manner that conveyed his appreciation for her honesty and integrity.

The President called for a press conference. With Eleanor and his legal counsel by his side, he stood before the nation and delivered his statement. He acknowledged the oversight, expressed regret, and outlined the steps he was taking to rectify the situation. He emphasised his commitment to integrity and transparency, hoping to regain the public's trust.

Following the public disclosure, various oversight bodies, including Congressional committees and the Office of Government Ethics, initiated investigations. The President directed his staff to fully cooperate, providing all requested documents and information. His legal team worked diligently to ensure compliance with all legal requirements and to address any issues that arose.

The initial reaction was a mix of shock, disappointment, and cautious optimism. While the media scrutinised every detail and political opponents seized the opportunity to criticise and demand he step down, many appreciated the President's decision to come forward voluntarily.

The President scheduled a series of interviews with major news outlets, where he reiterated his commitment to transparency and accountability. He also launched new initiatives aimed at improving financial disclosure practices and preventing similar issues in the future. This proactive approach helped to gradually rebuild trust.

Understanding the public's anger over the broader fraud scandal involving Peter Rainer, the President worked with Congress to create a relief fund for the victims. This fund provided financial assistance to those who had lost their savings and investments, demonstrating the administration's dedication to addressing the fallout of the scandal.

The President also championed new legislation to tighten regulations on campaign financing and financial disclosures for public officials. These reforms aimed to enhance transparency and accountability in government, addressing systemic issues that had contributed to the scandal.

The President's decision to confide in Eleanor and subsequently take responsibility for his actions marked a significant moment in his presidency. Eleanor's continued support and counsel were crucial in navigating this challenging period, underscoring the importance of trusted advisers in times of crisis. Beneath it all she knew The President had the ability to present himself as an honest man who had transgressed and wanted to put things right, and a manipulator, an actor who had the capacity to say and do anything and get away with it.

In the months that followed, the President continued to face scrutiny, but his proactive and what appeared to be a transparent approach helped to restore some measure of public confidence. The administration's focus on ethical reforms and support for fraud victims became a central part of its legacy, demonstrating a dedication to learning from mistakes and striving for a more accountable government. The President had been wounded but was not dead but mentally appeared to her to be enjoying the drama that he concealed from all those around him. He was unstable.

Eleanor felt a deep sense of foreboding as she arranged a private meeting with the President.

She knew him better than anyone, and the recent developments had revealed a side of him that troubled her. His vulnerability and mental fallibility were evident to those in his inner circle. He had been displaying erratic behaviour creating an atmosphere of fear and uncertainty in the Oval Office. She worried that without intervention, his presidency, and his mental health might spiral beyond control.

In the quiet, dimly lit setting of her office, Eleanor waited anxiously for the President to arrive. She had meticulously planned what she needed to say, balancing her professional duty with her personal feelings. When the President entered, she could see the strain etched on his face, his usual confident manner replaced by a look of defensiveness and paranoia.

"Thank you for coming Mr President," she began. "We need to talk. I'm deeply concerned about you."

The President's eyes narrowed, and he crossed his arms defensively. "Concerned about what, Eleanor? I'm managing everything just fine."

Eleanor chose her words carefully. "It doesn't seem that way to me, or to those around you. You've become increasingly isolated and defensive. Important matters are being neglected, and your behaviour is... troubling. " Before he was able to speak, she continued. "I understand what you have been through. I admire you for confessing. I admire you for your political tenacity to navigate your way through all this, you are a survivor, and you are still here to do the work you are so good at doing for the American people and for the world order.

I know you're under immense pressure, but shutting people out and refusing to lead is not the solution. You've always been strong, but even the strongest need support."

For a moment, the President said nothing, his expression unreadable. Then, his shoulders sagged slightly, tears flooded down his cheeks, and he sank into a chair. "I feel like I'm drowning, Eleanor," he admitted, his voice barely above a whisper. "Every decision, every action feels like it could be the one that ends everything."

Eleanor moved closer, her heart aching at the sight of his vulnerability. "You don't have to face this alone.

We can get through this, but you need to let us help you. You need to be honest with yourself and with those who care about you."

He looked at her, with a flicker of hope in his eyes. "But what if it's too late? What if everything comes crashing down, even now?"

"It's never too late to seek help and make changes," Eleanor said firmly. "We can start by addressing the immediate issues and then work on a plan to rebuild and move forward. But you have to trust me, trust us."

The President nodded slowly, a glimmer of hope returning. "What do you suggest?"

Eleanor outlined a plan that included bringing in a mental health professional to help him cope with the stress and his tendencies. She also suggested delegating some responsibilities to trusted advisers to lighten his burden while ensuring that critical decisions were still being made effectively.

"You need to reconnect with the people who support you," she added. "Show them that you're willing to face these challenges head-on, and they will stand by you."

The President's look of anguish changed; he forced a smile. He got up from his chair and hugged Eleanor warmly and she reciprocated. "Alright, let's do it. But, Eleanor, I need you by my side through all of this."

Eleanor smiled; her eyes filled with emotion. "I'm not going anywhere. We'll get through this together."

Over the following weeks, the President began to implement Eleanor's plan. With her support and the confidential help of mental health professionals, he gradually regained his stability and focus. He made a public statement acknowledging his mental health struggles and his commitment to transparency and effective leadership, which was met with a mixture of scepticism and support.

Eleanor remained by his side, providing the strength and counsel he needed.

Her love for him, though complicated by their professional relationship, became a source of resilience for them both. Together, they worked to restore the administration's credibility and to steer the country through its challenges, one step at a time.

She had accepted that she loved a psychopath, for he would always remain so, but managed, by her, the qualities he possessed could be harnessed for the good of the American people.

Over the following few months, and despite outward appearances of regaining control, the President's internal turmoil persisted. His public demeanour masked a deeply worried and introspective state sometimes leading to erratic behaviour and rash decisions. The veneer of confidence was thin, and those closest to him saw the cracks forming. It was clear he was on a path of self-destruction, and Eleanor felt a growing sense of urgency to intervene more decisively. She was by his side, but he felt alone, unable to control his emotions.

Eleanor watched with increasing alarm as the President's decisions became more unpredictable and damaging. Policies were announced without consultation, key advisers were sidelined or alienated, and long-term strategies were abandoned in favour of impulsive actions. The administration was in disarray, and Eleanor knew saving his Presidency was a tall order.

Eleanor gathered the President's most trusted advisers for a private meeting, sharing her concerns. The consensus was clear: a drastic intervention was necessary to prevent further damage to the presidency and the nation.

Together, they devised a plan to confront the President and persuade him to take a temporary leave of absence. During this time, the Vice President would step in, allowing the President to seek intensive mental health support and recovery.

Eleanor, along with a few trusted advisers and the President's personal physician, arranged a meeting with the President in the Oval Office. The atmosphere was tense, but Eleanor's resolve was firm. She knew that this might be the only chance to avert disaster.

"Mr. President," Eleanor began "We are here because we care deeply about you and the future of this country. We've all seen the immense pressure you're under, and we're worried about your well-being. We believe it's in your best interest, and the nations, for you to take a temporary leave of absence to focus on your health."

The President's face hardened, a flash of anger in his eyes. "I don't need a leave of absence," he snapped. "I'm perfectly capable of doing my job."

Eleanor stared at him. "We're not questioning your capability, but we've seen how the stress is affecting you. Your decisions have become increasingly erratic, and it's impacting the administration and the country. You have done a fantastic job during your second term, and we want that to continue until you step down at the end of your presidency. Please, let us help you. Take the time you need to recover fully."

The President looked around the room, seeing the genuine concern and solidarity in the faces of his closest advisers. His physician stepped forward, gently reinforcing Eleanor's plea with medical advice on the necessity of a break.

After a long, tense silence, the President responded. "Thank you all. I can see you have my well-being at heart. I will take time out at Camp David."

With the President agreeing to the leave of absence, the transition was swift. The Vice President assumed the duties of the presidency, and the President was taken by helicopter to Camp David where he could focus on his mental health.

During his absence, Eleanor maintained regular communication with him, providing updates on the administration and encouraging his progress. The Vice President, supported by the remaining advisers, worked diligently to stabilise the government, and implement the policies that had been neglected.

Months later, a rejuvenated President returned to Washington. His time away had allowed him to regain his mental balance and refocus on his responsibilities.

He publicly acknowledged the challenges he had faced and the importance of seeking help, earning a renewed respect from the public and his peers.

With Eleanor's support and the commitment of his team, the President embarked on a renewed path of leadership.

The administration worked cohesively to address the nation's challenges, and the President's experience became a powerful testament to the importance of mental health and the strength of seeking support in times of crisis.

Eleanor's love and dedication had not only saved the President but also helped steer the nation back on course.

CHAPTER NINETEEN

THE ASSASSINATION

As the President's term neared its end, he retreated once more to Camp David to reflect on his presidency's achievements and assess the effectiveness of current policies. It was a time for introspection, away from the frenetic pace of Washington, and an opportunity to contemplate the legacy he would leave behind.

Under his administration, the economy had seen significant growth. Tax reforms and strategic investments in infrastructure had created jobs and spurred innovation. The President took pride in the reduction of unemployment rates and the rise in household incomes.

One of the administration's major accomplishments was expanding access to healthcare. Through bipartisan efforts, the President had managed to push through reforms that increased coverage and reduced costs for millions of Americans. The implementation of telehealth services had been particularly impactful, especially in rural areas.

Despite initial resistance, the President's push for green energy had led to substantial investments in renewable resources. The establishment of new national parks and the enforcement of stricter emissions standards were seen as significant steps toward combating climate change and preserving natural resources.

The administration had invested heavily in education. Initiatives to integrate technology in classrooms and increase funding for research and development positioning the US as a leader in innovation.

While challenges had been numerous on the international stage, the President took pride in strengthening alliances and opening dialogues with adversarial nations.

The administration's approach to the war on drugs had been multifaceted, combining law enforcement with rehabilitation and education. While the legalisation of certain drugs in some states remained controversial, the data suggested a decrease in drug-related crimes and an increase in treatment success rates.

Immigration policies had been a contentious issue. The President reviewed the impact of measures aimed at securing borders while providing pathways to citizenship for undocumented immigrants. Despite progress, the policy remained a divisive topic, needing refinement.

The President had pushed for significant reforms in criminal justice, aiming to address systemic racism and reduce rates of reoffending. The impact of these policies had been positive.

While there were successes in expanding access to healthcare, challenges remained in controlling costs and improving the quality of care. The President noted areas for improvement, including mental health services and rural healthcare access.

Despite economic growth, income inequality persisted. Policies aimed at increasing the minimum wage and providing tax relief to the middle class had made strides, but the President acknowledged the need for continued focus on reducing the wealth gap.

In the solitude of Camp David, the President also reflected on his personal journey. He considered the trials and triumphs, particularly the crisis involving Peter Rainer and his own mental health struggles. These experiences had profoundly shaped the latter stages of his presidency, underscoring the importance of resilience, transparency, and the support of trusted advisers like Eleanor.

As he contemplated the future, the President penned notes for his farewell address, intending to highlight the administration's achievements and acknowledge the challenges that lay ahead for the nation and world order. He planned to emphasise the importance of unity, bipartisan cooperation, and the continued pursuit of justice and equality.

He also thought about his life post-presidency, considering how he might continue to serve the public and advocate for the causes he cared about.

The President understood that his legacy would be shaped by both his successes and his failures.

He was determined to leave office with a sense of fulfilment, knowing that he had faced immense challenges and had made tough decisions with the country's best interests at heart.

He returned to Washington to finish his term ensuring that the transition to the next administration would be smooth and that his policies would continue to benefit the nation long after he had left office.

As with so many things in life we are unable to predict the future. Upon returning to the Oval Office through the streets of Washington, the President stopped his bullet proof car and got out to greet the gathering crowds. The Security Services were adamant the President should not leave the vehicle, but he insisted.

While shaking the hand of an elderly man surrounded by his security team, a single solitary gunshot was heard from a distance, and in a split second the President immediately dropped to the tarmac in a pool of blood. There was panic, people screaming, rushing in all directions as security personnel surrounded the President as he lay there. Emergency services arrived in minutes rushing the President to hospital.

President Daniel Trent was pronounced dead on arrival.

Eleanor and the President's closest advisers were devastated. The country was in shock. News flashed around the world that another US President had been shot and killed while in office.

The President's assassination was a tragic and sudden end to a complex and tumultuous presidency. As he stepped out of his bulletproof vehicle to greet the crowds, his gesture driven by ego exposed him to a fatal threat. The sound of the gunshot reverberated through Washington, and in an instant, the President's life was extinguished, leaving the nation and the world to ponder what would happen next.

Eleanor and the President's closest advisers were struck by a profound sense of loss. They had witnessed first-hand the President's struggles and triumphs, and his death felt like a cruel twist of fate. In the immediate aftermath, they found themselves grappling with both grief and the monumental task of ensuring stability during the crisis.

There was an immediate vacuum in Eleanor's life. She had not just lost her President, she had lost the man she branded a psychopath, but a psychopath she had learnt to love. She would never recover from her loss.

The President's assassination reverberated around the globe. Leaders and citizens alike expressed their condolences and shock. Vigils were held in major cities, and people gathered to mourn the loss of a leader who, despite his imperfections, had strived to make a positive impact.

In Washington, a period of national mourning began. Flags were flown at half-mast, and a state funeral was planned to honour the President's service. The Vice President, now the acting President, addressed the nation, promising to uphold the values and goals of the late President's administration and ensure that justice would be served.

The immediate focus shifted to the investigation. Law enforcement agencies, including the Secret Service and the FBI, launched an extensive inquiry to identify and apprehend the gunman. The investigation revealed that the assailant was a lone individual with a history of extremist views and mental health issues. It became evident that the gunman had acted alone, motivated by personal grievances rather than a broader conspiracy.

Eleanor, amidst her own profound grief, played a crucial role in navigating the transition. She worked closely with the Vice President and the President's advisers to ensure that the administration remained functional and focused on its core responsibilities.

She also took on the task of preparing a tribute to the President, reflecting on his achievements and the impact he had made. Her speech at the state funeral was both poignant and heartfelt, capturing the President's dedication, struggles, and humanity. Her words resonated with many, offering a glimpse into the personal and professional challenges the President had faced.

Eleanor and the President's advisers continued their efforts to advance the causes he had championed, ensuring that his work would not be forgotten. They focused on implementing and expanding his key initiatives, particularly those related to healthcare, environmental protection, and social justice.

The President's assassination served as a stark reminder of the fragility of life and the unpredictable nature of fate. It highlighted the importance of safeguarding democratic institutions and the rule of law, even as the country grappled with the loss of a leader who had influenced its course.

In the end, the President's death was a profound and sobering reminder of how fleeting and precious life can be. It challenged the nation to confront its grief, honour its past, and continue moving forward with resilience and hope.

Back in the White House, Eleanor continued to serve with distinction in the Vice President's administration. When the Vice President was elected to the presidency, he remembered Eleanor's exceptional skills and the vital role she played. Valuing her political and diplomatic acumen, he offered her the position of Chief of Staff, a role she accepted with grace and humility.

As Chief of Staff, Eleanor was instrumental in shaping policy, managing the executive branch's operations, and providing strategic counsel. Her role involved overseeing the coordination of various departments, facilitating communication between the President and Congress, and guiding significant policy initiatives.

Her deep understanding of political dynamics and international relations made her a pivotal figure in the administration.

Eleanor's time in The White House was marked by numerous achievements. Her diplomatic skills were crucial in navigating complex international negotiations, strengthening alliances, and addressing global challenges. Domestically, she played a key role in advancing legislative priorities and ensuring effective governance.

Four years after President's Trent's death and nearing the end of the new President's first term, Eleanor suffered a fatal heart attack while chairing a meeting of advisers. Her passing was a profound loss to the administration and the nation. Her colleagues and the President were deeply affected by her death.

Eleanor's contributions were widely acknowledged and celebrated. Memorial services and tributes highlighted her impact on the country and the world.

Her legacy was recognised not only through the policies she helped implement, but also through the personal relationships she cultivated and the respect she earned from her peers as an honest broker.

Eleanor's achievements as a loyal public servant were significant. Despite the personal challenges she faced, including her deep grief over President Trent's death, she remained committed to her work and her adopted country.

Eleanor's life and career were defined by her steadfast honesty, upholding the truth at all costs. She was a highly intelligent and ethical human being born to serve with integrity and dedication. Her legacy would be a reminder of the profound impact that committed individuals can have on the course of history. Her work in the White House and her influence on international affairs left a lasting gift ensuring that her contributions would be remembered for generations to come.

Printed in Dunstable, United Kingdom